Fairytale to Meaning

LUKE SHEEDY

Author of Learning to Unlearn

Copyright 2022 Luke Sheedy

All rights reserved. No part of this publication maybe reproduced, stored in a retrieval system, or transmitted in any form or by any means, electronic, mechanical, photocopying, recording or otherwise, without the prior written permission of the copyright owner.

The author of this book does not dispense medical advice or prescribe the use of any technique as a form of treatment without the advice of a physician, either directly or indirectly. The intent of the author is only to offer information of a general nature to help the reader in their quest for inner transformation and spiritual well-being. In the event the reader uses any of the information from this book for themselves, which is your constitutional right, the author and the publisher assumes no responsibility for these actions.

Cover/Internal Designer: duosista.com.au

ISBN: 978-0-9874968-7-4

Fairytale to Meaning

LUKE SHEEDY

Author of Learning to Unlearn

For Me, a Nobody.

Persona *(Latin, "actor's mask"). One's social role, derived from the expectations of society and early training. A persona is useful both in facilitating contact with others and as a protective covering, but identification with a particular persona (doctor, scholar, artist, etc.) inhibits psychological development."*

James Hollis

Society tames the wolf into a dog. And man is the most domesticated animal of all.

Friedreich Nietzsche

Do what thou wilt shall be the whole of the law.

Aleister Crowley

The beauty of ones soul is all that matters.

To Mum and Dad, I love you both.

*To Kerrin, my loving sister, for
always watching out for me.*

*To Zara, my beautiful daughter,
you kept my light from going out.*

*To Louise Langford, true friendship is hard to
find so with you, I consider myself blessed.*

CONTENTS

Introduction 1

1. The Storyteller 9

2. The Lie 21

3. Sickness of the Soul 31

4. It's Your Journey 82

5. Our Stories 101

6. Halfway 120

7. Death and Rebirth 138

8. Be a Nobody 164

9. Meaning 183

10. Homecoming 177

Bibliography 182

> *We are literally a schizophrenic species.
> We are at war with our own nature.*
>
> **Terrence McKenna**

TO THE READER

Accept yourself as you are. And that is the most difficult thing in the world, because it goes against your training, education, your culture.

Osho

One of the challenges I have most days in private practice is to look into the eyes of those who have been beaten down and have lost their way from believing in an impossible fairy tale. Those lofty ideals and high expectations passed down to us by the storytellers who we have entrusted. To pass on much valuable wisdom and insight to endure the arduous task of living. It turns out it hasn't given us the desired affect we once had hoped for. Often our minds are filled with unhelpful phrases, presumptions and faulty beliefs. Things that have been seeded and wormed there way into our imaginations and naive minds at such an early age. Stirring up our emotions and anxieties, creating dysfunction and disorientation from our true self. For example, "You can be anything you want" "Work hard and you'll become a success." and, "If I can do it, so can you." Statements such as these are poisonous, to our minds putting us under a lot of pressure that can be out of ones reach. We feel like anything's possible and yet life's not like that.

Reflecting back on my childhood, it became apparent to me it's a part of the narrative of being socialised, following cultural, societal norms, and doing what's expected. Imitating, acting and believing that it's all probable to achieve and have anything we've ever wanted. It's a part of the process of being conditioned, to develop the ego to compete, strive and thrive, in a culture were the winner takes it all. We've all been bought up to be everyday hero's in our story but whose story exactly is it, and for what purpose. None of us are heroes, not really. We're just us.

Were surrounded by storytellers who inadvertently use their subliminal and direct messages of coercion to disempower and seek control over us. Whether it be our parents putting pressure on us to live out there unfinished lives through us or the digital media, making us believe everyone should look flawless, or we can have what we want and live a glamorous lifestyle. Clever marketing manipulates us to consume everything within arms' reach or television programming enforcing their idiotic, lofty, extrinsic values upon us. In turn this creates stars in our eyes and a subservient race addicted to materialism and a hedonistic lifestyle. Each year the bar gets raised and the measuring stick becomes way too long, manipulating our insecurities. Creating enslavement to our anxieties and neuroses, conjuring up feelings of despair, guilt and shame.

The discord between who we ought to be and who we actually are widens. Our lives get turned into soap operas and it's not until the reality of living my life and listening to the stories of others. That I began to realise there's so many forces which are outside of our control. Our place and regardless of how important we believe we are, there's a much more powerful force in life that can disrupt the best laid plans. As the saying goes, "Man plans, God laughs." With time and age, I've drawn to my own conclusion that we're all just tiny, minuscule spots in such a wide, vast universe.

Throughout my counselling career, I've come to the professional opinion that many people have held this narrative. That for them to live meaningful and successful lives they must believe and adhere to an impossible fairy tale. Sadly this generates disenchantment for most people creating stress, disconnection and guilt. A sense of failure becomes the moral of their story, when their journeys don't conclude to a fairy tale ending.

Reflecting back on my own experiences, I believe I have had to become more emotionally and mentally resilient to what life gave me. Life has a way of tempering my inner muscles to strengthen my inner core and by accepting many truths which have derived from my own direct experiences, life has taught me some very humbling lessons. Which are don't believe in the storytellers fairy tales, which had misinformed me from the very beginning. Deluding me that I could have my cake and eat it too.

Unfortunately we all get mislead to believe that the storytellers, are the final arbiter, but as we get older we soon realise it is all rubbish and the storytellers don't know anything. Your beliefs, experiences, truths become a part of your own story. And not the myths, fables and legends which have been passed down by those we have allowed, considered and believed in. But if you go ahead and absorb and swallow everything to what you've been told, seen or heard. It will become a detriment to your psychological health and story.

"Psychological health will be the leading health concern in the western world by the year 2030," states the world health organisation. That's not a myth or a fantasy but a fact. The majority of people believe in the storytellers rhetoric and imprison themselves between the four walls of their minds. Believing, imitating and following through with orders which have led most of us down the garden path of a fictitious story. Unfortunately the storytellers leave out the most important part of the story, subjective reality. That is, no two individuals can experience reality from the same perspective. There are many subjective realities as there are sentient beings. We all because of our dependency and lack of consciousness, resign our deepest stories intended by the Gods, and trade them in for the provisional stories that our reading world around us provides.

In a modern world full of distractions, coping mechanisms and technology, we must always be focused on the constant, sudden and severe. We must always remind ourselves how important it is to remain still, open and have reconciliation with outside forces. Regardless of your reputation, social status or bank balance, ultimately your life is in the lap of the Gods. Or just maybe we get so caught up in a rhythm of expecting from ourselves, more than our talent and character can supply.

The message that lies between these pages is far from a fairy tale. But the reality of living one's life in a toxic culture such as ours were the majority believe in the storytellers fairy tales. That, we can be anyone, look perfect, enjoy absolute health, buy all the shiny toys, and do anything our heart desires. Unfortunately reality is not like that, as the majority of us will eventually find out for ourselves.

The only way to begin and rewrite your story is to shine the light of truth to what is reality and what's fantasy. Fairytale to Meaning has powerful consequences which will empower you to live your life from your own narrative. "Insist on yourself, never imitate," said Ralph Waldo Emerson. It's time we all become more responsible for ourselves and get in touch with our own existential core.

This is your story and you must be responsible for your life. It's no longer the storytellers rhetoric and ideologies that get to write your life's script. Our society has grown sick at its attention to the outlook of surface living lifestyles and shoddy values. From now on you must look within and listen to the small voice that can be heard by you alone. It's time to live the story that you have been summonsed. Everyone has a story, just make sure it's your own.

Love always,

Luke

FAIRYTALE

A fabricated story, especially one intended to deceive.

Luke Sheedy

PREFACE

The unforgivable sin is to choose to remain unconscious.

Carl Jung

We try and live our lives the best way we can. Unfortunately we take on other people's faulty beliefs, concepts and templates from those we've loved and held in such high regard. How can there be a one size template fits all mindset? There isn't, believing if we listen and take on the cultural standards and societies wisdom, it'll be beneficial to us and enrich our lives. What if a lot of what we've believed to be true isn't, but a fairy tale and a generational disease passed down throughout the ages. My way to deal with this is don't believe anything. If you believe in something, you are automatically precluded from believing its opposite. Knowledge is provisional to the person who experiences it and can have a devastatingly effect on how we live and interpret our lives and the choices we make.

Everyone gets socialised at an early age by their parents and from our society to get us ready, to live. In a culture were the theme is to believe that our lives must be lived a certain way. Which will guarantee you happiness and a fulfilling life. Unfortunately these are the fairy tales which I'll be referring to throughout this book. The messages we receive from the storytellers contribute to our unhappiness and frustration. Communications via social media, TV, movies, billboards and magazines promote the importance of things like, having wealth and material possessions, being popular, having lots of friends, career success, having a high-status, well paid job, a beautiful body or happy, harmonious, family relationships. People buy into these messages to different degrees. The more strongly we hold our beliefs, the more likely we are to feel unhappy when our life circumstances don't live up to them. For example, if you believe that you must have happy, harmonious family relationships, but in reality your family relationships are dysfunctional. The belief that things shouldn't be this way makes you feel miserable or inadequate. While there is no problem with preferring to have happy family or intimate relationships, beauty, lots of friends, achievements or material wealth, believing that things must be a certain way is guaranteed to create unhappiness.

We get told by those authoritarians that good overcomes evil, we'll find our soul mate, work hard enough and you can achieve anything, get married and you'll live happily ever after. Those that have caused us harm will be punished and you'll be vindicated from those who have sought out to harm you. This my dear readers is called a just-world theory and a faulty cognition, prescribed to us by the storytellers.

By the time this book will be complete I'll be forty-eight years old and have lived long enough to come to the realisation that the storytellers I believed, have spun me a tall tale. That's how this book became into creation. From my own life observations, experiences, and the witnessing of close friends and clients who have all been burnt out and disillusioned to the shit we all ate up when we were young and naive. The majority have a strong desire or need to believe that the world is an orderly, predictable and just place. As this narrative creates a sense of security, predictability and familiarity, so we all go about our daily lives believing we are in control.

Life isn't a fairy tale and it's far from just or easy. The more mature you get the more you realise that life just isn't like that. Arseholes thrive, people get away with bloody murder, the person you once held so dear turns out to be a nightmare. Someone you don't even know can destroy everything you have worked hard for within a blink of an eye and get away with it. The majority of people just go on believing everything they hear, see and read because they haven't been taught to question, challenge, or query authority. This in its due course will cause an identity crises and misinterpretation on how to enjoy the experience of life. Especially to those who have believed the storytellers rhetoric.

Life's full of shit heaps and shame, and nothing is ever black and white, but it's amazing how many people believe that it should be. Obedience was the golden rule taught at school and outside the classroom not autonomy, which has created a subservient race. That's why so many people are easily influenced and manipulated from the beginning of their lives and come halfway, find everything they were told to believe, turns out to be a fairy tale. Buddha said, "Life is suffering" and when you've lived long enough, you come to the realisation that there's so much of our lives which are out of our control. That we must just accept, surrender and respond in accordance to what's in our control.

Looking back over the faulty beliefs and rigid concepts, I've had the displeasure of hearing and reading now makes me laugh. We all find ourselves in this circus, were most of the clowns thrive. But when were younger it all seems so possible and plausible. The guy gets the girl in the end, all your hard work pays off, get married and you'll live happily ever after and if you have enough talent, fame and fortune will be your reward.

It's only natural and in our nature that we want to seek wisdom, learn and imitate those who seem to be successful, happy and fulfilled. But soon we all realise that not many of us are destined for greatness. And that we all walk different paths from those around us. No one has it all together, or has it all figured out regardless of how attractive or popular they are. Or how much money they earn, what car they drive, what suburb they live in or how many followers they have on Instagram. There's always a story behind a story.

We've all been led to believe in a fairy tale and what constitutes a happy and meaningful life. Unfortunately these extrinsic motivations all lead to a surface living lifestyle. Splitting us from our true self, creating disconnect from our true core and each other. In time and with a certain amount of age and maturity one would hope, but not all ways. We come to the realisation that real meaning comes from what you value and what you want your life to stand for.

Within our own society, children are born into poor families, have fewer life opportunities than those who are born to wealthy families and people on low income have poorer health and higher death rates from all causes than those who are well-off. Look in any large workplace and you will find talented, hardworking employees who are poorly rewarded and sometimes discarded while others in senior, well-paid positions may lack competence and dedication. Callous individuals are often not held to account for bullying or intimidation of fellow workers. Individuals with good looks, sporting prowess or the ability to make people laugh receive special treatment and privileges that are not available to the rest of us. Injustices exist within each society, every family and workplace. Even the very system created to uphold justice in our country is inherently unfair, try taking someone to court without a big bag of money to pay your legal bills. Perhaps we should be taught from early in life that many things are simply not just. Sometimes we need to accept that we live in an imperfect world, full of imperfect people and situations. The common theme in all of those fairy tales told to us by the storytellers is our expectations and lofty ideals will be met, if we just imitate, adhere and do the work. This belief, develops from an early age and it's only a matter of time in the near distant future do we realise it's a farce. And in due course begin to take off those rose coloured glasses and stop believing in those utopian ideals which have never matched our reality. It's only a matter of time we all come to the conclusion that we've all been deceived.

Believing in societies messages, becomes very demanding to our physical and mental health. How we see ourselves and who we think we must be. Unfortunately it's nothing but a viscous cycle of false substitutes, put there by the puppeteers that subdue us and seek control over us. Keeping us all caught in the web of delusion that we can be anything if we just try hard enough and persevere. This delusion will always be out of one's reach as that's all a part of the plan to keep us chasing but never arriving. Creating false hopes, broken dreams and burnt out people. As William S. Burroughs states, "What does the money machine eat? It eats youth, spontaneity, life, beauty and above all, it eats creativity. It eats quality and shits quantity."

It's only a matter of time that you'll come to a stage in your life that what you've believed to be true is false and in the end you'll feel betrayed and confused. If you don't start living life on your own terms, self-reflect and take responsibility and accountability by asking questions and challenging everything you've had the displeasure of believing. This will be the antidote to living a life more suited to you. Otherwise you are only setting yourself up for a robotic, meaningless and empty lifestyle. In the end nobody has the faintest clue to the truth of what life means, or what the mysteries are. All the truths you've been told could be the biggest of lies you can be sure of it. Best to learn from your own direct experiences, as they become your beliefs and not the lies of the storytellers.

I have met many people who have lost themselves trying to live the impossible fairy tale. I must congratulate all of my friends, acquaintances, strangers and clients who have been courageous enough to open up to me or have come to therapy for analysis to discover parts of themselves that they thought they've lost. Only now to rediscover how to live a more authentic, meaningful life according to their originality. I want to acknowledge those brave individuals who sought help and understanding to let me into their private lives from which I have gained valuable insight and the permission to use that information. Which has been used to create this book. In the end we all must follow our own lives as consciously as we possibly can. To realise our journey itself is symbolic, from Fairytales to Meaning and in the end, a great wonder to the mystery of life.

There comes a day when you realise turning the page is the best feeling in the world, because you realise there's so much more to the book than the page you were stuck on.

Zayn Malik

Fairytale to Meaning

INTRODUCTION

Everyone is born great but the process of living disables their greatness.

Unknown

By the time we have hit midlife, most of us are burnout, disappointed and cynical. We feel for a major part of it, life hasn't been good to us and we've fallen short. The storytellers fairy tales haven't lived up to our experiences and expectations once promised. In hindsight one can honestly say, the juice wasn't worth the squeeze and we become at odds at which way to turn in our lives. The results achieved never gave us the happiness, or gratification we'd once envisaged nor expected. We thought that by obtaining a particular identity and achieving a certain level of success. It would grant us a certain level of happiness. But what we realise is, it's only momentarily pleasure. The saying, to the victor goes the spoils becomes obsolete, a truth once promised, becomes a lie. A direct consequence of our naivety, a subservient behaviour learnt at an earlier time. We become obedient to appease what we thought would give us the recognition and validation we were desperately seeking. But in doing so we became less autonomous and more defined by our culture, which are boundary defining engines. As Terrence McKenna said, "If you are not careful, you will end up living the illusions others have created for you."

Out of our own fears and insecurities we try and control others to keep ourselves comfortable in our known part of the world, to stay safe and keep everything predictable. But to live life like this seems ridiculous, as there's so many variables and outside influences to disrupt our fairy tale mentality. We practically burn ourselves out trying to keep up with the social game. So once we get a degree, get the corner office, get married and live up to the standards planned for us, we begin to realise that were no happier than before we started. We've fallen into a trap of trying to live up to society's ideologies and what is to be considered normal. Yet the downside of appeasing others and playing the game, is we find out that the life we're living is not our own.

Life is very complex and complicated, there are so many variables vying for our attention that we have to consider to keep our dreams alive. Life isn't black and white, but many shades of grey which causes many people a lot of instability and confusion. The majority of us have followed some type of perfectionist mentality, which we believed would make us happier and successful. However it only creates inner emptiness, suffering and an all or nothing mindset. We're like rats on a wheel, chasing and striving to get ahead of everyone, yet burning out as a result. But what we don't realise, our lives are to be enjoyed in the moment and lived only now. Which will create a more meaningful happier life experience. So it's not about waiting for retirement or to have ones ducks all in a row. As fate may not grant you that wish, and your health just like everything else is impermanent and in a constant state of flux. The faulty beliefs and what we were once told, don't actually turn out to be the truth. As no one has that power to predict any ones future or how it should be lived. In the end we all learn the truth in direct consequence of living our own lives and not the fairy tales, we've all been subjected to.

I'm past the lunch time of my life and have been dealing with my own fairy tales being shattered and how ironic is it to have my own existential crisis at the time of this book being written. The slander of my reputation, separation of a long term marriage, the upheaval of my award winning business and having only two weeks to vacate the family home and find a new home whilst losing everything I own materialistically, due to flood waters. I'm always following my heart as I journey along my path. But there's a major part of me at times which feels disillusioned with the direction my life has taken. We all get told we can do or be anything, believing in fairy tales. If we knew what was up ahead of us in life and the shit we have to deal with, none of us would ever begin. But it takes courage to live life and get the most out of the experience.

I've come to the realisation, that I actually find myself a very fragile part of a small picture in a much vast universe. Regardless of how much effort, control or talent I believe I have. We're all at the mercy of uncontrollable forces which play a much larger role on the outcomes of our lives that we don't like to admit to. The whole fairy tale story that you can be anything or do anything, all of a sudden becomes a delusion and this is where the fairy tales which were imposed to us as children come into question. The biggest questions we all must ask as we get older to gain clarity and sense of it all will be, "What are we all doing here?" and "How do we find meaning in own lives, regardless of what we've been told or led to believe." "How do I start living more authentically?" is a question worth answering.

So the title, "Fairytale to Meaning" was often a phrase that I'd quite frequently use in therapy at work and hear myself repeating quite often to strangers, friends and family. The feeling of powerlessness and impotence, the vulnerability of the forces which play out in our lives which leave us by surprise and irrevocable conflicted with our own sense of purpose and who we are and what our lives stand for.

The title definitely hits an existential chord due to a deep recognition of our inner frustrations and resentment of the lies we've been told and believed throughout our youth and into the first adult years. I knew as a free thinker and writer, I was onto something exciting and profound. Which would later manifest into this book, which now rests in between your fingertips.

It's totally mind numbing how most of us have swallowed from time to time the ideals, unobtainable standards and high expectations which have been handed down to us by the storytellers. Domesticating us with their ridiculous fanciful notions and shitty values. It's definitely a generational and culturally disease. It's not hard to find the fallout of these fairy tales, when we're all suffering under this torturous fantasy in which we've all been pressured to believe and adhere to. It's a fantastical story no doubt, it's so far from the truth which disconnects us from living one's own reality. Creating neurotic behaviour in all of us to help us cope with living the absurdity of the day to day narrative in a mad world.

But what we all fail to realise in the beginning to a significant extent, are the combination of faulty beliefs, stories, self-concepts, philosophies, superstitions, lies, ideologies and mistakes. All from those struggles of flawed people that we get stuck with at the very beginning of our lives. The planting of impossible seeds that germinate into our subconscious and eventually appear later in our lives, producing our narratives and how we move through life, stumbling blindly through believing the unbelievable, medieval and mythical.

The culture, with its ideologies and power mongers, the marketing giants to a large extent which influence us, devoted to wickedness with their crimes of deception. They tells us with their idiotic values, what a person should be, what we should look like, how we should behave and live. We internalise these rules, then begin adhering to them as if they are the rules of the universe. They are all the scoundrels who constitute the evil agency in the plot of our life stories, which becomes a major obstacle to our own self-knowledge and flourishing life to what should be our journey.

We start to feel an emotion of revulsion because we don't have the big house, look like the ideal shape, you don't drive the latest sports car or have the high flying career. Or travelling to exotic places for vacations every year, that's our culture talking. You've absorbed it, it's inside of us and we become a part of it. To a significant extent, it controls us, like a parasite, admonishing you when you stray too far from its models. We're about ninety per cent of our culture and that's what we are. We become cogs in a much larger machine.

Unfortunately, we've believed the story who we are becomes our internal monologue and that little voice that keeps us in check and interprets everything that's happening to us. It discusses what's working and what's not and it never shuts up, creating inner turmoil and the suffering of daily life. We mustn't remain a prisoner of our childhoods any longer if we wish to see ourselves as living authentically.

Depending on how mentally flexible you are it might just serve you for a while. You might just create the identity in which you wish to play out with these particular characters in your mind. You fulfil those roles that the culture wants you to believe, the socialite, the entrepreneur, the breadwinner, the successful athlete, the award winning business owner. This creates your persona and the illusion that you're keeping up with certain roles, responsibilities and expectations, which you believe you have to follow. To fit in and keep up with the ideology that keeps us enslaved to the mirage for things and illusions of status and class which makes us chase. Having to get to the next level to make us feel better about ourselves. While the inner wounds fester for a life we're not even destined to fulfil, alienating us from our true natures and those we love.

That's the perception of the fairy tale in which we've all been deceived in by the storytellers. It becomes a fools paradise, playing out these little roles, looking for validation and approval wanting to conform and play the game. All lying to ourselves and each other because we want to avoid our inner pain, but in doing so we hugely damage ourselves of inner peace and meaning. We lie about how much effort it would take to alter our jobs, relationships, our health, habits, ideas and lifestyles for something more appropriate. We all need to think well of ourselves and devote to imagining that we're essentially normal. As most people in society want to be somebody in a world full of nobodies. Fooling and lying to ourselves is the prerequisite as we don't want to feel so inadequate.

But what happens when what we perceive to be happiness and what we perceive to be reality is in actual fact a fairy tale, a much part of a larger mould to keep us controlled. What happens when the fairy tale ends or fails? What happens when we no longer see ourselves as the heroes, but now the modern day losers or worse a nobody. You see we've all been lied to, is it really apart of the human experience to believe we all have so much control? In all areas of our lives, career, relationships and health, and how you perceive yourself and others and the character you build along the way.

We kid ourselves that we're doing well, and go along with a template that is incredibly dysfunctional. This is what society wants and expects of you. You've become a product of social perfectionism and your self-esteem will be in danger if you can't maintain those standards and expectations. The fairy tale becomes a nightmare, when our mission stops, or worse ends. The expectations, ideals and events of our lives, all fall short of those pie in the sky ideals and roles we act out to appease others that look on with great interest ready to judge with shame and ridicule. We feel defeated, resentful and humiliated. It feels like we can't escape and we lose faith in the capacity to change internally and externally. Suddenly we become shrouded in darkness giving up with lifeless abandon, like someone or something has covered up over the picturesque colourful world which we thought was once ours. The eerie reality for a much darker sinister one begins. The certain clear belief and vision we had for a prosperous future, now has become a dark and stormy nightmare. The feeling of melancholy is such a heavy burden one now wears. Depression and anxiety take hold of us like an unwelcome visitor in the dark, the fairy tale ends. The bar has been set way too high in an unimaginable fantasy in which we've all been led to believe. Life becomes a disappointment and feelings of confusion take hold. We've all taken on someone else's story because we didn't know how to write our own.

But are we that free to choose what direction to take and mould our lives to how we feel we should live, or is it the storytellers power and right to tell us what to do. Are we just leaves on the freeway of life being blown around by much larger forces beyond our control. The difficulty begins with the levels of aspirations which have become so high on the basis of overly exaggerated notions of free will. We deem everything about our lives capable of change, through our own actions and behaviours. Usually we declare that we can achieve all things through our exercise of free will.

Unfortunately this cannot always be the case and the results can be radical under achievement and self-deceit, or when things don't work out as sure as day follows night, one's life will turn to bitterness, cynicism and rage. The debate has been long running between defeatism and determinism. Each of us needs to decide for ourselves whether we believe everything is predetermined or of our own conscious volition.

Or maybe we should all handle our lives like Friedrich Nietzsche called, "Amor Fati" translated from Latin as a love of one's fate. To accept everything which has happened in one's life, not to erase anything from the past, but rather accept which has occurred the good and the bad. No longer spending time regretting or lamenting the unfortunate twists of fate and wishing things should and could of gone different way, but to believe it is what it is and to do the best we can with the cards we've been dealt.

Seems more plausible to surrender, embrace and stop fighting the inevitable. Maybe we are all headed to a degree of catastrophe from the start, but we do have to say yes to life half with horror and the other half with ecstasy to the whole of life. We are a civilisation suffering spiritual amnesia on a colossal scale. We've forgotten who we are and how great we can be. Instead of believing the ghosts of the past, we must tune into the Gods that live within each and every one of us and live accordingly.

This book is an opportunity to re-examine your own life and ask yourself about the roles you've pretended to play to appease others, but have left you feeling empty and disoriented. My purpose is for you to look back through your life and see how you've got to where you are now and to reclaim your life and live more authentically. Giving you an opportunity from this moment on to redefine and reorientate your story rendering it more meaningful and immeasurably richer.

From my own experiences and the counselling of others is that the capacity for our growth depends on our ability to internalise and to take personal responsibility. But to also have the ability to detach from those events, occurrences and results out of one's control. If we forever see our own lives caused by others, a problem to be solved, then no change will ever occur. If we are deficient in courage, no changing can occur. Life is a double edge sword in its absolute horror and occasional moments of awesome beauty. We maybe powerless to alter certain events but we may remain free to choose our attitude towards them and an unprotesting acceptance of what is truly necessary that we can find a distinctive serenity and freedom.

But many of us treat our lives as if they were a novel. We pass from page to page, passively assuming the author will tell us on the last page what it's all about. As Hemingway once said, "If the hero does not die, the author just did not finish the story." So on the last page we die, with or without illumination. My mission in this book is to help you become aware and accept responsibility for the rest of the pages in the story of your life. And to risk the largeness of life to which you have been granted.

So much of our story was written by fate, so much written by others. At least some small part of it, perhaps the best part, is yet to be written by us. And the souls hour, this hour we inhabit now, asks of us: And how will you write your story from this hour onward?

James Hollis

THE STORYTELLER

At every moment of our lives, we all have one foot in a fairy tale and the other in the abyss.

Paulo Coelho

Our lives are a story and what we perceive, becomes who we are and who we ought to become. Yes, we're all born free, bearing the germ of wholeness and health, and then life happens. Since children are dependent upon their parents and their culture for the fulfilment of basic needs, they are quickly estranged from their natural being. We are all socialised to serve and maintain the collective, family structures and social institutions that have a life of their own, but require the repeated sacrifice of the individual to sustain them.

At such an early age we have our impulses, urges and instincts curbed by our parents, educators, religious institutions and society that we've been immersed in to. The majority fit in and comply and do as there told as not to ruffle any feathers and follow the herd mentality. This is the beginning of a tale that gets woven into our lives by the storytellers who tell us what's expected and what should be adhered to.

We all want to feel like we belong to the group and back when we were hunters and gatherers it's either you stuck within the group and did what you were told or were seen as a troublemaker. To be alienated, was the punishment and you would die alone in the process. Nothing has really changed as all individuals today are still seen as dangerous and ostracized. As Plato said over two thousand years ago, "Those who are able to see beyond the shadows and lies of their culture will never be understood, let alone believed by the masses." So to this day the majority go along with the psychologically enslaved mentality. Which creates self-consciousness and the seeking of validation and approval from those very storytellers and loved ones that squeeze the very authenticity out of us and into the social stream of conformity.

We form groups and start to develop prejudices and biases. We become preoccupied with what others think about us, as most believe their sense of self is a reflection of what other people think about them. As we spend more and more time with others we start to develop hierarchies.

Within these hierarchies comes our obsessional concern with status. We constantly seek validation. Why do we buy the fast cars? Why do we buy the big yachts? Why do we buy these things we don't really need? It's because were signalling to others of our self-status. If others believe were fancy and great, our looking glass self-interprets that as evidence that we are fancy and great. We're all so self-conscious, we use clues from out there to tell us who we are in here.

To realise the way we view ourselves and our reality depends wholly on the extent of our own experiences and truths. When we're born we are handed multiple lenses, genetic inheritance, gender, a specific culture and the variables of our family environment, all of which constitute our sense of reality. As John Locke said, "Parents wonder why the streams are bitter, when they themselves have poisoned the fountain."

Sooner or later though, we have to admit that we have perhaps lived less from our true nature, than from the vision of a reality ordained by the lenses we were handed out when we were younger. We begin to acknowledge the partiality of the lens we were given by family and culture was already fixed and set through which we made our own choices and suffered their consequences. Maybe if we had been born of another time and place, to different parents who held different values, we would have an entirely different lens and ultimately different lives.

The life we received generated a conditional life, which represents not who we are but how we were conditioned to see life and make choices. It's fascinating to witness how we defend our vision of our story, our world as superior to that of others. So too, we succumb to the belief that the way we have grown to see the world is the only way to see it. The right way to see it, and we seldom suspect the conditioned nature of our perception. It's not until we wake up and become conscious of our inner discretions that project a faulty and rigid way of living life and seeing life from a different perspective. Even in the most privileged of childhoods, I have noticed people believe they have experienced the most traumatic of early childhood.

We were connected to the heartbeat of the cosmos in our mother's womb. Suddenly we were thrust violently out into the world to begin in exile and a search to recover the lost connectedness. The initial experience of the world is devastating to our sense of self. Some of us will become the sociopaths, and the character disorders who will fill our prisons and haunt our streets. The majority will roam blindly living someone else's life and only the courageous will become self-reliant and individuate.

Close to half of the western world will suffer from a mental disorder throughout their lifetime. Many people will go onto experience a feeling of emptiness and lack of meaning due to what they have obeyed and believed to be true. From the stories we've been socialised and subjected to. The beliefs and behaviours that we've been told, prescribed or witnessed from such an early age become the walls we confine ourselves in and within this rigid structure, shape our reality.

So in many ways, we can't help but experience our lives as a story and it's not only the work of the confabulating interpreter that's responsible for this. Because of the way our brains function, our sense of me naturally runs into a narrative mode. We feel as if we're the hero of the steadily unfolding plot of our lives, one that's complete with allies, villains, heroes, nobodies, monsters, rescuers, sudden reversals of fortune and difficult quests for happiness and appraisals. Although we do have our tribal brains which cast haloes around our friends and plant thorns on the heads of our enemies. But to experience our stories as cause and effect we have what is called the episodic memory and it interprets everything as a sequence of scenes.

However, the autobiographical memory helps us imbue these scenes with sub-textual themes and moral lessons. We're constantly moving forward, pursing our goals on an active quest to make our lives, and perhaps the lives of others somehow better. To have a self is to feel that we are the invisible actor at the centre of our world and that we're in control. But are we? Or maybe there's a larger force, playing our hands for us which we have no control over?

Our biased brains ensure that the invisible actor which is us, seems like a good person, someone who is morally decent whose values and opinions are usually correct. But whose beliefs, opinions and concepts are they? Those of the storytellers or who we are. We like to think our lives have a pattern that's heading in the right direction towards the perfection of our potentials, although we do suffer from setbacks almost all of the time which are from outside forces out of our control. Which we go on to blame someone or something.

In our stories and the lives that we lead, we do believe we're heading in the right direction getting better and closer to a fairy tale to which we have been led to believe is true and possible.

But the happy, healthy mind is rather mischievous and sly, running a gamut of sly tricks in order to help us feel that we're in control. It ensures that were often over generous with our estimation of ourselves, imagining we can do anything as this is what we've been led to be as true. That we're better looking, kinder, wiser, more intelligent, have better judgment, are less prejudiced and more effective in our personal and working lives than is actually true. Virtually every one of us irrationally inflates our moral qualities to see ourselves in the most beautiful of one's own light. Whilst throwing shade on those around us. I guess our egos really are the enemy.

Only a minority like to have intrinsic motivations which lead to a meaningful and purposeful life. Only the right values in one's life, will lead to a more enriching and colourful experience. Giving one a sense of accomplishment of doing something worthwhile. A monument of character maybe better than a legacy of a concrete structure that holds no meaning or value.

But then there are the majority who have believed in the ideologies that more is better and it's never enough. With their extrinsic motivations, such as pay, status, fame and fortune, job security and to have the body beautiful and a glamorous lifestyle. Oh how let down they all become when they've been led to believe that instant gratification and status is the portal to instant happiness and success. If this were true why are so many celebrities and successful people today, who have achieved a level of what our society deems as success, are having to cope and deal with a great deal of depression, anxiety, emptiness and loneliness. A majority of celebrities are now expressing to their fans and followers, that seeking fortune and fame isn't what it's all that cracked up to be. As Jim Carrey the famous comedian and actor said, "I think everybody should get rich and famous so they can see it's not the answer."

So our minds at times can be great storytellers as well and it can see itself as a hero, antihero or nobody. Which becomes the role you play and live out on a day to day basis. So which one are you? The hero, nobody or antihero as it makes out the plot and shapes your life around what it believes to be true. As Oscar Wilde said, "We are all in the gutter, but some of us are looking at the stars."

The mind is a plagiarist, stealing ideas from the stories that surround it. From our parents, television programs, family environment, the education system, digital media, culture, the government and the religion we get subjected into since birth. These are your storytellers which give you a beginning to your life stories and create your tunnel vision reality who I'll be referring to throughout this book. To me, they all can be at certain times be the villains of our lives and unique stories.

For example as children we often receive messages from our parents, "Be successful and you'll become happy." "Get a good job that pays well." But so many parents do this because they project their unfulfilled lives onto their children. So there's this added pressure to succeed and children experience the love of the parents as conditional. It can be a very fine line between lovingly protecting and nurturing a child, or living through the child inappropriately.

When the parents own life has been blocked by anxiety for example, the child will find it hard to overcome barriers and may even get stuck in an unconscious loyalty to the Parents level of development. But a parent who is living his or her own life is not unconsciously jealous, nor projecting their fairy tales, or expectations onto the child. So the child will feel naturally open to self-discovery to live their life in their own unique way, with their own unique identity.

Many parents are disappointed in their children because they didn't go to the right college or marry the right person, or perhaps because they don't espouse the right value system. Their disappointment is in direct proportion to seeing the child as an extension of themselves and not as a different being with a unique path of its own.

If you truly love your children, the single best thing you can do for them is to individuate as much as possible yourself, for this frees them to do the same. We should treat our children worthy of being different, having no obligation to us whatsoever. They are not here to take care of us, we are here to take care of us.

Whether our parents feel guilty for not being the perfect parents or just seeking to protect us from the trials of life, it does not serve us well. The desire to control through lies to have them live out their incomplete lives, and to replicate their value systems which is not of our own, is not love but narcissism and it impedes our journey. Naturally, the parent or primary caregivers are often the children of incomplete parents and can only model and transmit his or her own experience.

The two greatest needs of a child are nurturance and empowerment. Nurturance implies that the world will serve and meet us halfway, support and feed us, physically and emotionally. Empowerment implies that we possess the wisdom to meets life's challenges and to fight for what we desire. But what happens to us when these challenges, desires and expectations aren't met?

Unfortunately how many of our parents are consciously aware to stop this from happening? Many of us had wounded parents who could not meet our needs for nurturance and empowerment. So we have had to struggle to be ourselves and we often wish our parents had recognised that we were meant for different paths from the outset, but they didn't.

So we absorb their stories and values that flow from their mouths and into our minds and we use them to make sense of our past, our future and to help us figure out who we are and who we want to be. We use them to construct our narrative identity and how we're going to live and play out our lives.

It's the stories that our parents tell us which shape our characteristics and personality. As children, these stories told begin to play a part in building our understanding of ourselves and our lives. The Jesuits said, "Give me a child between zero to seven and I'll shape the man." This is the age where all the programs of our beliefs and concepts all get indoctrinated into our subconscious mind and we actually run off ritually and habitually throughout our entire waking state. Until we become aware enough to realise we've been told a fairy tale and build up enough courage to change.

As a child, you believe what your parents tell you. The content of these stories, including ideas about cultural roles, institutions, our relationships with our parents and values, start to emerge with our sense of who we believe we are and who we should be and act in society. This becomes our conditioned self. But sooner or later you're going to start to realise some of the stuff they taught you wasn't right and doesn't fit in with your core values and true nature.

It's during adolescence that we start to understand our lives as a grand narrative. In order to help build this narrative, our memories of the past are shuffled, warped and edited as if by a canny screenwriter who turns us into a sympathetic, heroic or antiheroic character. We also start imagining the future in such a way that it fits the story we're creating.

That silent little voice inside each and every one of us all becomes the narrator of our own story and from all of those who have played their part in influencing our fertile, naïve and precious little minds. Before too long one is not aware of the impending danger of the seeds which have been planted, and they begin to sprout and strangle our individuality and originality. Causing rigour mortis to those that don't shed water and light onto their own experiences and truths.

From the distorted beliefs and rigid self-concepts that we can be anything or anyone are simply fairy tales. We hear them as children from our parents or primary caregivers who are the main storytellers. As well as religion, government, our education, to films, digital media, works of literature, advertisements and news stories that portray the world more directly. To ancient holy books, stories work as both entertainment and a kind of shopping mall of the self.

Culture provides each of us with an extensive menu of stories about how we ought to live, and each and every one of us chooses from the menu. But we become caged by our cultural programming and imprisoned in the tiny pedestrian world of consumerism, with its materialistic values which places a barrier between our egos and our true nature. If you go against the ideology of culture it creates a certain kind of alienation between you and others, creating a sense of shame and guilt. The culture teaches you we do it this way, don't ask questions or go there in your heart. If you follow the rules and how it operates which is all about control you are choosing to limit and disempower yourself and the journey you take.

We build our sense of who we are by the appropriating stories from our storytellers. Turning our lives into myth and something which further along the path comes to an abrupt end, realising we can't have everything we want, achieve the ultimate goal or get to the next level of success because life is not like that. Our stories give our lives meaning and purpose, but it also distracts us from the chaos and hopelessness from the dread of truth.

That to play the game of life and to live and immerse yourself in it, you're going to have to give up your originality to fit in if you wish to succeed and play your role well. To play your character role in this fairy tale you're going to have to develop many personae roles which are necessary fictions. To fit and comply with the storytellers lies, faulty concepts, superstitions, bias, prejudice and rigid templates which take up a lot of our energy to appease them.

We are one with our parents, another with our employer, friends and a different one with our partner. Our conditioned self, warps and morphs depending upon what it believes is expected of it. It's amazing how many of us complain when visiting family events such as Christmas and we seem to helplessly revert back to our childhood selves. This is because mum and dad are treating us as the person we were. As we travel through our daily lives, then, we're being continually changed and challenged by the situations we're in and the personalities that orbit us. The people around us create a kind of psychic mould that we expand into.

Unfortunately to go along with the fairy tale we lose ourselves in the process and who we truly are becomes a distant memory. Sure our masks become a necessary interface with the outer world, but it does create confusion with others and with our own inner truth, values and how we perceive ourselves and unfortunately the majority end up believing they are the roles their actually playing. This in time creates a split of who we truly are and the suppression our authentic nature. This creates disharmony of who we are and a loss of one's way. If who we are to a significant extent is our culture which is composed of the slim, prosperous, happy, extroverted and popular. This is what our cultures believes that we're all supposed to be. We see this person everywhere, in advertising, in the press, and all over social media.

The human world becomes a game in which we all compete with each other, with the most deserving winners taking the spoils. These people become the victors who play the heroes that society and the culture look up to with their extrinsic values and who now are nothing but empty shells of their former selves. Most sell themselves out to the cultural engineers rubbish values and shit brain thinking. They've had to redefine who they are for the convenience of a particular story that they pay homage to and this involves narrowing down direct experience of living and a denial to be ourselves. Causing such distress and disconnect it creates a sickness of the soul.

But this model that gets impressed to us daily is extremely dangerous. People are suffering under the torture of this impossible fantasy. Unprecedented social pressure is leading to increases in depression and suicide, because of all the shame and guilt that social perfectionism creates.

Unfortunately we've believed a lie and have trusted the storytellers to tell us how our lives should be and lived out. But the problem with this is our character roles change and when they do, we experience a loss of our own identities and who we thought we were, creating spiritual emptiness. The feelings of disconnect with our authenticity and the essence of oneself and the interconnected tapestry of a much bigger story to one's life and our place in it.

It becomes a major disappointment and disruption to the fairy tale that the storytellers have spun us. Chaos thrives between our socialised self and our authentic self. A split occurs which creates neurotic behaviour because a lot of people can't accept themselves for not being able to reach the high pedestals which have been raised too high by those who have been writing a horrific script.

Were constantly told we're not special, so we look for guidance, support and mentorship. Looking towards the storytellers, believing they have all the answers and they'll give us direction and a larger purpose. But it's really you who has the final say on your journey and you will be the final arbiter, and if you take responsibility for your story you'll be less infected by the storytellers lies, manipulations and deceptions. But the majority go along with it, and that's a terrible idea with horrific consequences.

The only way to break the storytellers spell is not to believe in their misconceptions and rhetoric. But to live your own life and not somebody else's. To go by your own heartfelt individual experience, which in turn creates your own journey towards meaning and an enjoyable story. This is your life and it shouldn't be in the hands of anybody but yourself. It's your time to have your place in the sun, move into the light and walk your own path.

But too many people believe and give away their authority to the storytellers that write the script and just accept what they've been told. Committing themselves to ideologies, which are just exposed as a nice story which seek to maximise control and aren't interested in your life, or your authenticity. Unfortunately we betray ourselves and we cluster around any storyteller which we believe will lead us out of ignorance and into the shining light of truth is ludicrous. The culture and the institutions turn us into robots and we believe they have power and control to do so which creates a form of infantilism and this unwillingness for all of us to go it alone, be alone and be ourselves.

We from the very beginning give our lives and power away, but we must all realise that culture is provisional and so are the storytellers, who weave their spells of deception. Yet even in this day and age we are yet to approach this understanding. We must reject authority and the storytellers that spread their falsehoods, it's leading us into ruin and it's not real. Don't believe me? Take a look around you and the mental state of the inhabitants of western civilisation. The majority have become alienated from themselves, no longer having a sense of reality or truth.

So it's up to you as you're the main player in your life as the hero, anti-hero or nobody of your journey. You have to make a decision based on how you want to live your life and what you want it to stand for. It's either you congratulate yourself for challenging and questioning what you get told and go by your own direct heartfelt experiences and live within that. Or you can get fed someone else's bullshit and keep being led astray, by the storytellers.

Not to know one's true identity is to be mad, disensouled thing – a golem. And, indeed, this image, sick-eningly Orwellian, applies to the mass of human beings now living in the high-tech industrial democracies. Their authenticity lies in their ability to obey and follow mass style changes that are conveyed through the media. Immersed in junk food, trash media, and crypto fascist politics, they are condemned to toxic lives of low awareness. Sedated by the prescripted daily television fix, they are a living dead, lost to all but the act of consuming.

Terrence McKenna

THE LIE

The simple step of a courageous individual is not to take part in the lie.

Aleksandra Solzhenitsyn

We've grown up enmeshed with the falsehoods of the storytellers that were all supposed to be amazing, and live these grandiose lives. Making and portraying us to believe that we all can do anything, be everything and make the improbable possible. The outcome of all this fantastical thinking is we all end up having stars in our eyes. We get put into this hypotonic state that the world and life really is our oyster.

The majority end up with these delusional fantasies that they are more relevant, important or powerful than they truly are. They have inflated self-esteem and overestimated their powers and beliefs which, in later years of life, becomes a very unpalatable stew for all who have observed, swallowed and digested the storytellers poison. We have all been spoon fed by those we believed who we thought knew better than us.

An array of obsession and greatness surrounds us everywhere we go and we can't escape it. The films we watch, the advertisements on billboards, on the television and all across the social platforms and internet. The majority of people feel pressured and convinced in some way into living up to this fairy tale, which only breeds insecurities, false hopes and break downs.

We often fail to realise that the things we believe in are to a significant extent, a combination of faulty beliefs, rigid concepts and misconstrued stories. Which have been passed down through the generations with their superstitions, lies, mistakes and faulty templates. From flawed men in women with their own insecurities and neuroses. Voices from long dead people haunt us in the present, often without our conscious awareness replaying over and over the lies that run on autopilot within our psyches daily.

This was prescribed to us daily before the age of seven and became our rituals, routines and patterns of daily living. The beliefs that we haven't even questioned or challenged become our thoughts that constantly plague our minds. These faulty thoughts never shut up because we don't ever feel that we measure up, creating insecurities which make us sick to our inner core. We give other people too much power over us on what we should think and feel. How we get treated by others makes or breaks us. The majority feel immobilised by other people's expectations and demands. We become so co-dependent on how we should behave with those around us, that everything we do is somehow a reflection of our sense of self. Sacrificing our freedom and giving our powers away to the imposition of any authority, ideology, government, religion, culture or any other storyteller. This makes us take refuge in anything that we believe will make it easier for us. But there is a price to be paid.

Which is to say we are who others say we are. We're in this constantly evolving feedback loop, created out of our actions and other people's perceptions of our actions and our assumptions of their perception. It is how the majority work through this convoluted house of mirrors attempting to find and live with their true self. But living a lie to be a part of the herd mentality can be very stressful and painful. Why don't we all just be authentically ourselves? But that's too hard and risky, so it's easier to settle, live a lie and go along with what's expected.

It's all the arguments they've made, feuds they've waged, battles they've fought, revolutions they've triggered, industries and movements they've raised up. Destroying the millions of lives that have been decimated in the name of ideology, dogma and indoctrination which lives within each one of us. We all have so many people occupying space within us, that there's no more room. Our personalities are no more than the crowd that takes up free rent within us. We are a walking crowd of others all vying for our attention at any given moment of our waking state. Being pulled in many directions, yet not a path of our own.

Of course we all have different versions of who we are by our experiences, gender, age, family, job, spiritual beliefs, our pasts and the way we interpret those experiences. But it's not hard to detect the general model of how perfect we all should be and live up to these unrealistic standards to find happiness and be successful. We all must follow our dreams and if you dream big enough you'll discover that anything is possible.

But as we grow up we begin to learn that what we've been led to believe as true, becomes only a fable. We start to lose sight of what was once a fairy tale and that anything's possible, becomes extremely odd and dangerous to those that have believed in it. The main plot of the story is that we're all responsible for our own fates, or so we tend to believe and we can be anyone and do anything, but this is the brutal and underside of the story which constitutes an evil agency in the plot and the villains we encounter along our journey.

These storytellers end up being the malicious people or agencies that are out to destroy and control the human individual experience. Soon enough we begin to learn, usually around halfway of our lives, that we're not talented enough, opportunities just don't arise and all the effort and discipline you have won't amount to much. As it was stated in the Bhagavad Gita when God talks with Arjuna, "You're in control of the amount of effort into your labour, but you're not in control to the fruits of your labour." Leaving Arjuna feeling very disgruntled and weary.

The tales we believed to be true, end up just becoming myths and the majority of us feel like dismal failures to those of us who once believed them. What we took on as fact, has now become fictional, robbing us of our hero status and when our progress stops or comes to a grinding halt. From playing this character we've developed and devoted our time believing in, it all makes us feel so inadequate and disengaged. Our mental health takes a direct hit, creating inner despair, meaninglessness and disorientation.

The demand for everyone to keep up with the fairy tales, becomes such hard work. Which is to keep up with the social pressures within our society. The cultural engineers which have devoted their time and power to this wickedness are out to maximise control. To such degree that if we commit ourselves to any storyteller, we become poisoned by it.

> *Soon after we begin living we become aware of the confines of our prison. It takes us thirty years at the most to recognise the limits within which our possibilities will move. We take stock of reality, which is like measuring the length of the chain which binds our feet. Then we say: "Is this life? Nothing more than this? A closed cycle which is repeated, always identical?" This is a dangerous hour for every man.*
>
> **Jose Ortega Y Gasset**

The lies in which we once believed in by those trusted, have found out to be tall tales from the storytellers around us and the culture that sets the stage and agenda. Our culture is not our friend and how much of who you truly are has been repressed to stay in line with the story and the plot which we've been led to believe is the only game in town. It's a fictitious tale spread by neurotic individuals, which has always been a collectivized consensus about what sort of neurotic behaviours are acceptable.

As Terrence McKenna said, "Culture is the convenience of culture, how many times have your sexual desires, career aspirations, relationships, the true authentic happiness of who you are and what you really wanted to do with your life has been squashed, twisted and rejected by what you've believed to be true, with the cultural values that you adhered to which has lead your life into total disarray and confusion."

The storytellers fabrications and the culture have all defined who we are, what our lives should be, how we should live, and what success is and how it should look like. They have told us and teach us you do it this way, not like that, you can be happy if you buy this, follow in my footsteps and you'll achieve great success. Anything's possible if you really want it badly enough. All of these words and phrases which are used, are loaded with empty promises and fruitless dreams preying on our insecurities and desperation to fit in and be successful.

So if you have acted on this fibs and played by the rules you've chosen to limit yourself to someone else's story line and not your own. We give our own journeys to celebrities, icons, faulty beliefs, templates, fictitious stories, and the so called successful lives of others and it's time to stop consuming these falsehoods of the culture and begin to live our own lives, our own way. No longer believing in what we once were incessantly told.

But a major obstacle to self-knowledge and in turn to a flourishing life is the tendency that we have is to lie to ourselves. We lie because we want to avoid pain, but in doing so we hugely damage ourselves of achieving happiness. We lie about how much effort it would take to change our jobs, our relationships, our friendships, our health habits and ideas. We need to lie to think well of ourselves and become totally devoted to imagining that we're essentially normal, without peculiar love, hates and devilish thoughts. We lie because we don't want to feel so inadequate and yet because we lack so many good things. We have to be the master of our own deception and our techniques are widely deviant and often highly imaginative.

We all have sides of ourselves that we hide. We have things that we do and like, that we are ashamed of, things we don't understand or can't seem to control. No one exists without vices, without flaws some traits so unpleasant and off from the shared game of normality that sometimes we can become insufferable to those who get close enough to us. As a result, most of us survive socially more on the surface rather than displaying the more complex and difficult elements of who we really are, in order to fit in and enjoy more social interactions.

It's perhaps reasonable, to some degree to play along with the social game and to withhold some heavier dark information and qualities of our self. Rather than burdening others with our dysfunction, very well knowing that everyone else is also dealing with their own. However there also needs to be a place and opportunity to access, share and connect over these dysfunctions for the same reason. Be it that everyone is dealing with them but rarely is anyone sharing or talking about them.

More about this in the next chapter. We spend so much of our life trying to contrive and live as the best versions of ourselves in the minds of others. That we become totally lost or in an estranged state of conflict over who we really are or who people really are.

Here are some ways we like to pull the wool over our own eyes. We identify with something that can powerfully keep our thoughts away from our troubling confrontations. Online pornography is a favourite, risqué behaviour, excessive exercise, gambling, the news another, alcohol and work. Anything that impedes you from seeking the truth, resistance really is the devils' advocate. As Friedrich Nietzsche stated, "Alas, I have known noble men who have lost their highest hope, and henceforth they slandered all high hopes. Henceforth they lived imprudently in brief pleasures and they had hardly an aim beyond the day. Once they thought of becoming heroes: now they are sensualists. The hero is to them an affliction and a terror. But, by my love and hope I entreat you: do not reject the hero in your soul! Keep holy your highest hope!"

We don't so much like these elements in and of themselves, we like them for their ability to keep us away from what we fear. A sadness we haven't been able to admit to is often covered up with exaggerated doses of manic cheeriness. We aren't happy as much as incapable of allowing ourselves to feel even the slightest sadness, in case we were to be overwhelmed by our buried grief. We develop a brittle tendency to say that all is very well, I'm okay or it's all good.

We might press to any ideas to the contrary. Denied anger with a particular situation often seeps out into a generalised irritability. So successful is the lie we don't really know what's up. We just keep losing our tempers, anything can just set us off. Our lives are so filled with how frustrating and annoying things are. We have cleverly left no space at all for focusing on the true and very sad issue.

We simply tell ourselves we don't care about something, love, relationships, creative outlets, hobbies, politics, career, success or intellectual life. The beautiful sunrise or the house we can't afford and we are very empathetic about our lack of interest with complete disdain. We go to great lengths to make it very clear to others and ourselves how unconcerned we are.

We grow censorious and deeply disapproving of certain kinds of behaviour and people. What we don't admit is that we're so full of condemnation, only because we need to ward off awareness that a part of us, in fact really likes the condemned element. We attack certain sexual tastes as utterly deviant and beyond the pale, precisely because we have known to share them, somewhere inside ourselves. So we're delighted when particular people are arrested or shamed in the press. What they did was utterly awful we think, shielding us from any risks, spotting the connection between them and us.

Feeling offended takes up a lot of our attention and it muddies the waters. We no longer pay attention, that our heart is correct, but challenging. Were sad about particular things but confronting them would be so arduous we generalise that it's a universal sadness.

We don't say x or y made us sad we say everything is rather terrible and everyone is rather awful. Our sadness gets metaphorically lost in the crowd. As Soren Kierkegaard said, "There are instincts that protect themselves against attackers by raising a cloud of dust. Likewise man instinctively protects himself against the truth by raising a cloud of numbers." Better to do what everyone else is doing, than to be yourself.

Whether we are aware of this or not, no matter how rich or famous, smart, attractive or powerful anyone may appear on the surface, we all share in this. But we're all seen as broken, confused and flawed, perhaps even more than those who praise him. Rather than hiding or being dishonest about the struggle we all go through it. It's the sharing of our experiences of this struggle with authenticity and honesty that helps us uncover it. So we can face it and grapple with it and hopefully transmute it into something beautiful or helpful. But how many of us are willing to share ourselves with complete vulnerability and authenticity or at least try.

One of the dictums that defines our culture is that we can be anything we want to be, to win the game all we have to do is dream, to put our minds to it, to want it badly enough. This message leaks out to us from seemingly everywhere in our environment: at the cinema, in heart-warming and inspiring stories we read in the news and social media, in advertising, in self-help books, in the classroom, or television. We internalise it, incorporating it into our sense of self, but it's not true.

It is in fact, a dark lie at the heart of the age of perfectionism, which the storytellers have been weaving. It's the cause, I believe, of an incalculable quotient of misery. Here's the truth that no million-selling self-book, famous motivational speaker, happiness guru or blockbuster Hollywood screenwriter seems to want you to know. You're limited, imperfect, and there's nothing you can do about it. And no matter how hard you try there are some things we're not that good at, some ways of being we just can't master. Regardless of all the promises we might make to ourselves and our loved ones. There are personal qualities we'd all love to have, but unfortunately we can't make it stick.

One of the most surprising things I've come to realise is that storytelling is a form of tribal propaganda. Just as our hunter gatherer ancestors gossiped about selfish and selfless people. It all helped to control the tribe, by teaching its members to be the selfless heroes, rather than the beaten, ostracised villains so the same mechanisms exert powerful social pressures today.

So we make the tribes story our story. We spread it around, in our own gossip and we've believed in the storytellers, becoming unconsciously complicit in the conspiracy. And then we try to become this hero, forcing ourselves into shape, in the gym, at the office, or on the therapists couch. All too often we fail. When the plots of our lives stall, when they fall short of those unobtainable standards and high expectations, we can't see a way back to feeling heroic then dangerous perfectionistic thinking can be triggered.

We eventually may decide that we're losers at the game. We feel self-loathing, we might even find ourselves contributing to the already terrible statistics on suicide, depression, self-harm and eating disorders. But what these stories don't tell us is that it's all a lie. None of us are heroes, not really. We're just us. Everyday nobodies and that's okay just to be well, ourselves.

It's only when we lose the fights of our lives and keep on losing that we become stuck and humiliated, broken heroes, enemies of our evermore demanding culture. Then the story that is our self, starts to fail. It begins to creak and crack and the actual truth of what it is to be a living human presses in on us.

All we have ever wanted was the illusion of control. But we have none, not really, and neither do the people around us who seem so happy in all their radiant perfection. Ultimately, we can all take comfort in the understanding that they're not actually perfect, and that none of us ever will be. We're not, as we've been promised, 'as Gods' but fallible humans.

So why is lying to ourselves a problem? We need to tell ourselves the truth, and just be us, otherwise we often pay a very high price for the short term calm of our lies. We miss out on key opportunities for growth and learning and we become not very nice people to be around and we develop harmful conduct, which goes against what it means to be us. When we don't let our true selves emerge, it has a tendency to reveal itself through involuntary often physical symptoms. We suffer from insomnia or become impotent. An eyelid starts twitching, we acquire a stutter, scream in our sleep and lose energy. We become addicted to substances that are foreign and harmful to our very being, squeezing the very essence of who we once were out into the abyss of the in between states. We try to escape this world which we currently inhabit, from a plethora of coping mechanisms and distractions creating sadness and emptiness. At our core nature this is not who we are, but this world is powerfully and tragically geared to causing a high background level of anxiety, sickness and mental instability. The story of the modern world has a way of making the majority of us all psychologically unwell which in turn creates a sickness of the soul.

Above all, don't lie to yourself. The man who lies to himself and listens to his own lie comes to a point that he cannot distinguish the truth within him, or around him, and so losers all respect for himself and for others.

Fyodor Dostoyevsky

SICKNESS OF THE SOUL

When the average person cannot hide his failure to be his own hero, then he bogs down in the failure of depression and terrible guilt.

Ernest Becker

Depression is a universal sense of feeling vulnerable, in which we feel disempowered and at a loss to who we are, or what we're here for. That feeling of not being good enough. The majority feel like nobody needs them or have any interest in them. We feel like our lives and our true selves are being ignored and that's humiliating. So this becomes our existential dilemma, the fundamental problem for us all is that we want to overcome death, and because we can't but we want to, we literally do it symbolically.

How? Through the meaning we give our lives, this then becomes our story. Unfortunately the stories we've been told are fairy tales which demand illusions. As you know sooner or later illusions fall apart, turning into vapour corrupted by people who intentionally or unintentionally like to wreak havoc out of their own self-interests. It's an invisible hand we come to realise, that controls and manipulates the scripts of our stories.

Depression is a form of disconnection, where we feel that we've been separated from something that we need, but also have lost along the way. We've become utterly disconnected from ourselves, pursuing happiness as that's what we've been taught by the storytellers is to chase after the next goal or shiny object never enjoying the journey so therefore we never arrive. As a direct result and a response we become too exhausted and don't ever feel any closer at achieving what we have our hearts set on. Not being able to meet these expectations of our cultural demands divides us. Raising a bar each year which keeps getting moved every time and makes it tougher and rather impossible for anyone of us to achieve or maintain.

We all live the first half of our lives in service to essentially a social agenda, namely, the task of developing sufficient ego strength. To leave parents, venture into the world, commit to obligations, partner up, serve citizenship roles, create security, status and create the world that is expected.

> *Advertising has us chasing cars and clothes, working jobs we hate, so we can buy shit we don't need. We're the middle children of history, man, no purpose or place. We have no Great War, no Great Depression. Our great war is a spiritual war, our Great Depression is our lives. We've all been raised on television to believe that one day we'll be millionaires and movie Gods and rock stars. But we won't. We've slowly learnt that fact and were very pissed off.*
>
> **Tyler Durden, Fight Club**

By believing in the fairy tale we've given away our freedom to others and act in accordance to the storytellers modus operandi. We have to free ourselves from a set of habits that once promised us a symbolic victory over others and our deaths. As it now seems so empty and destructive. These demands cause a lot of grief and shame creating major imbalances with our mental and emotional health, instilling the generalisation of guilt and shame.

This shame makes us sick, which unfortunately seals off everything which is good about ourselves and we draw to the conclusion that we're disgusting and it poisons our very lives right down to the roots. It's even harder if you don't have a supportive partner or friends. Your chances of developing a mental illness is seventy-five percent higher, if you don't have a sympathetic network.

But how does the sickness of the soul actually occur that we feel so disconnected in the first place. To who we really are, what we've been led to believe and what in life really matters. The majority of us have a house fire burning inside of us, but unfortunately we only concentrate on the smoke until life becomes so intolerable to bare and everything we thought was so important turns to ashes.

We form our sense of identity, from baby to adolescent and young adult to the person holding this book now by what the storytellers have told us. We go along with the play and act accordingly to what's expected of us until eventually the fairy tales and our reality don't match up to a grain of truth. Causing confusion and conflicts within us. This causes neurotic behaviour were we go out looking for all types of coping mechanisms, gambling, drinking, partying, risqué behaviour, anything that stops us from getting to the bottom of our feelings of discontent and frustrations. These distractions we use to counteract our feelings of lack of self are just dopamine hits, which just give us instant gratification yet keep us away from healing. But after we've had our fix we go back to the same base line of feeling not good about ourselves or worse before we gave into our cravings. Our feelings of lack and loathing get repressed deep down into the subconscious mind, which becomes the shadow self or inner demons. This shadow or our demons are the parts of us, we hide from the world because we feel they make us seem ugly or despicable. As the story we've been told makes us feel inadequate to what seems appropriate to someone else's story. It's not until we meet and face our demons will we be able to turn our nightmares into meaning and become whole. As Dante Alighieri said, "The path to paradise begins in hell."

But we become socialised into the main plot to live in a way that doesn't meet our psychological needs, so we get left with a sense of despondency. The messages from the storytellers have deliberately absorbed us into their junk values since the day we were born. We form attachments to our primary caregivers beliefs and those we admire and respect, seeking their love and approval rather than our own. So we begin to distrust our own instincts, impulses, secret wishes and after enough time we forget who we are and what's important to us. Out of all of this our egos have been constructed to make us compete, divide and rule, while repressing our authentic self, deep down into the cavern of the subconscious mind.

Our constructed self or ego becomes our new sense of self which becomes a reflection of what we want others to think of us, and because of this we become self-conscious and inadequate to ourselves. We become strangers to ourselves and to those around us.

> *"I am not who you think I am;*
> *I am not who I think I am;*
> *I am who I think you think I am."*
>
> **Charles Cooley**

The whole narrative is based and set up to get us to think and act this way. Get the grades, get the best paying job, rise through the ranks and display your earnings through your house, clothes and cars. There's that part of us that thinks, if you keep buying stuff, people on the outside observing you will think you're a success and so you will yourself to be happy. So that's how we pretend that every things fine and to make yourself feel good. The funny thing is though it's not the spending itself that makes us happy and acquiring the object of desire. But getting to the psychological state that makes us feel better. The dopamine hit is very addictive, but yet very costly to what's really important.

Spending our way to happiness is toxic, as it numbs the emptiness, but doesn't fulfil it. These junk values distort our minds and lives. The whole logic of our culture tells us to stay on the consumerist treadmill. To go shopping when we feel lousy and fill up on the emptiness inside of us with new toys. The advertising that surrounds us makes us all feel scant and we get offered products to solve our inadequacy for us, because we deserve to be this person and if we don't we get the message were no good without it.

Advertising is a form of mental pollution that directly or indirectly contaminates our minds. The culture creates a picture for you of what you must look like, creating unrealistic body standards and there's immense pressure to achieve a perfect body, thus deteriorating our overall self-esteem and creating unhealthy habits.

We're taught happiness is to buy something, show it off, display your status, acquire things and it's all being drummed into us from advertising and social interactions. Children want to belong so you buy the branded clothes so they'll be accepted by the group and get a sense of belonging. The narrative of the storytellers is if you buy this thing, it'll yield you more happiness and respect. The culture primes us to compete and compare, which is always a thief of joy.

People on Instagram and Facebook flaunt their delusion of self-importance, which only ever shows one percent of their actually lives and you must ask yourself why? Why do they do that? They're just seeking validation and acceptance. Aren't they're just searching for reassurance, due to their deeper feelings of inner lack and low self-esteem, in a need just to be exalted. While the majority just slander, gossip, and judge others anyway to make themselves feel better out of their own feelings of self-doubt and unworthiness. Isn't this what most people like to do, pull others down to lift themselves up. Social media will never replace or compensate psychologically for what we've lost to real intrinsic human connections and the reality of living our lives with honesty and authenticity.

All these junk values lead to an increase in self-doubt, low self-esteem and a plethora of mental illness. The storytellers train us that there's never enough money, status or possessions. More, more, more is the anthem from the capitalists. Your boss tells you to work more and you think I've got to work more because my self depends on it, my status, my wealth and achievements, as it all gets internalised becoming an internalised oppression.

The shit you buy, ends up owning you and it's never enough. All the external goals accomplished never return day to day positive returns when they've been fulfilled. It's just the same after a while and your happiness doesn't improve an inch. The need to satisfy the desire for things requires a lot of energy which affects our lives in a negative way. Creating and occupying a lot of space in our minds and disempowering our sense of self.

Do you love me for my house, car, job or handbag, I'm an executive now at work, have I happen to mention that I've just bought a holiday house. We become hollow and exist in other people's reflections. A lot of people are advertising made visible, products of a consumeristic culture. We do what the storytellers have been priming us to do since childhood. Work hard, play the game, compete, live a lie believing in the fairy tale that materialism and shitty values is the answer, which will make your life meaningful. It's a materialistic society set up to reinforce materialistic values and in the end cripple our internal satisfactions. This alienates us from ourselves and we become a part of the collective whole. It's always better to be loved for who you are, than to be admired for what job you do or what you have.

For thousands of years philosophers have been suggesting that if you overvalue money and possessions or if you think about life mainly in terms of how you look to other people, you'll be unhappy. It's a known fact that people who are more object-orientated have more levels of depression and anxiety. As they have bought into the fairy tale that happiness comes from accumulating material possessions and believing a superior status is everything. The more you do something for applause and effect the more you can't relax in the moment. As your ego is always searching to improve, be stronger, larger, healthier, richer and will never shut off. The nervous system goes into overdrive and survival mode, creating burnout of the hormonal glands which secrete toxic hormones, called cortisol. These hormones circulate around the blood stream, creating high blood pressure and heart disease. We all have a part of ourselves that is always comparing and judging looking at ourselves, over monitoring and over thinking.

If the culture we're embedded in isn't healthy you're going to end up with an unhealthy individual. As Jiddu Krishnamurti said, "It is no measure of health to be well adjusted to a sick society." The whole plot of the fairy tale is for all of us to forget our true selves, intuitions, instincts and our deeper connections with ourselves and each another. It's also to recognise that we're all one, in the higher aspect of life and that we all belong to a larger family of the human tribe.

We have all been raised to divide, conquer, compete and compare. The lives we lead are all caught in a system that wants power and control over our stories. The storytellers aren't about enlightening you. It's all about disconnection from a very young age against your authentic nature and enslavement to the matrix of the machine which is cold and heartless keeping you in materialistic bondage.

The ego is developed at such a young age within the first three years and it takes over, making us spiritually homeless, disconnecting us from others and ourselves. The ego shrinks us and our sense of self and so we buy to accumulate things. Our egos protect us, they guard us and are necessary to live in our society, but not when they become a detriment to ourselves and our way of living. We do need our egos to live here otherwise, if I took you to a restaurant I'd end up feeding you and forgetting to feed myself. But when the ego gets too big, it cut us off from the deeper meaning of connection, with who we are, others and the contract we are summoned to fulfil. The West is all about the Individual and the building up of the ego. In the East it's all about the collective and making things better for the group, hence why depression in Eastern culture, experiences fewer mental disorders.

We're good at meeting our physical needs, but not our psychological needs. The storytellers told us a fairy tale and we have disconnected from each other, ourselves and what matters most, interpersonal connections and a true relationship with our core values. We have lost faith in the idea that there is anything bigger or meaningful than ourselves, so the majority accumulate more and more objects of their desires.

Rare is the individual who goes through life without at some point being afflicted by a gut wrenching pain with the disconnection from their true self. Sometimes it's triggered by an adverse or tragic event, usually around the second half of life. But it's merely a reflection of the discrepancy between how our life is and how it could have been and what we've been told it should be. This casts a shadow over our very existence. For most people these feelings prove temporary, the dark clouds that feel so consuming in the moment lift, almost spontaneously and life resumes on course. But for others these feelings of loss and confusion don't abate with time but only intensify and mental illness settles in.

One comes to view themselves as worthless or an object of pity, hate and anger. Our lives can become a burden of the greatest magnitude. The question as to what leads people into the depths of depression has been debated for millennia. Why can some people recover quickly from adversity while others with similar circumstances endure prolonged durations of suffering.

Over the past several decades there has been an increasing focus on the biological causes of depression. But while our genes and biology may predispose us to depression, there is no denying that how we choose to live and behave are also of great importance. Not all lives are equal, if we wish to avoid the acute suffering associated with depression by relying too heavily on a limited number of sources for our feelings of self-worth.

As humans we have a basic need to feel that our life is of value and that we are here on earth not merely to take up space, consume resources and ultimately to die. This need to think well of ourselves and to have others do the same is one of the fundamental shapers of our life. For without feeling that we are an individual of worth we suffer and so much of what we do is driven to satisfy this need. The job we take, who we associate with, the status symbols we adopt and the social issues we champion are all influenced by whether they help or hinder us in this regard. The more sources we have to which obtain our feelings of self-worth the better. But some people often by the virtue of their upbringing greatly restrict themselves in this regard and in so doing they predispose themselves to mental illness.

For depression is often a combination of many factors, the loss of a valued object in conjunction with psychological rigidity. Which is the inability to produce a variability in our patterns of thought and behaviour and another can be to creatively adapt to changes in our environment. Our risk for both of these factors increases the more we rely on one or a few objects for our feelings of self-worth. In some cases people rely too heavily on another person, such are the individuals in constant need of the praise from a parent or a spouse to feel good about themselves. Rather than believing they can imbue their life with meaning and become an individual of worth through self-directed action. Such people always seek assurance, direction and validation from what can be called their dominant other.

But while those who live like this may have a good reasons for having slipped into such an existence, unfortunately this way of life never cures what ails them. For the more we rely on another person to validate our worth the more psychologically rigid we will become. We will never cultivate the crucial ability to attain self-esteem through our own effort. Discovering how to feel like an individual of worth without the constant praise of another is a necessary life skill. For if one's dominant other dies or abandons them, the lack of this ability will quickly take its toll in depression, sometimes of a severe nature. Or as Ernest Becker aptly put it, "Such a person has lost the only audience for whom the plot in which he was performing was valid, he is left in the hopeless despair of the actor who knows only one set of lines and losses the one audience who wants to hear it."

No man can wear one face to himself and the other to the multitude without finally becoming bewildered as to which may be true.

Hawthorn

In other cases, rather than relying on a dominant other some people adopt grandiose life goals in the hope that one day they will achieve such goals and this becomes the primary source of their self-worth. This tactic is often resorted to by individuals who lack satisfying interpersonal relationships.

Perhaps such a person grew up with emotionally distant parents, was ostracised by his or her peers or experienced too much rejection later in life. But whatever the case if one repeatedly fails to find the acceptance of others eventually he is likely to believe that there is something fundamentally wrong with him.

He must become someone else if he is ever to become worthy of the love and respect of others. And what better way to do this than by accomplishing a magnificent feat. Such as becoming a famous musician, a best-selling author, a successful entrepreneur or something else of a grandiose nature. Believing that one day we will accomplish this goal and therefore find the acceptance that we so desire can imbue our lives with meaning and help us feel that we're individuals of worth. Or at least on a path in the right direction.

But like the life lived in the service of a dominant other, this way of life places one at a great risk for depression. The problem it must be stressed is not the focussing on a single goal as often we need to limit our goal so as not to dissipate our resources. Rather the risk for depression arises because we stake too much on the achievement of any single goal especially if the goal is of a grandiose nature. Some may achieve their grandiose goals the majority don't and as the years pass. The goal remains nothing but a fantasy, the realisation eventually sets in that it is unlikely that success will ever be achieved. Therefore like the individual who's dominant other dies, so to those who stake their existence on the achievement of a dominant goal also experience a death. But in this case, it's the symbolic death of the individual they hoped to be and also who they've been told they can be by the storytellers.

When the ambitious man whose slogan is either Caesar or nothing does not get to become Caesar, he despairs over it. But this also means something else: precisely because he did not get to be Caesar, he cannot bare to be himself.

Soren Kierkegaard

But no matter how we go about limiting the range of sources from which we obtain our feelings of self-worth the problem is the same. When we lose the object on which we staked our well-being on we will be at a loss of where to turn.

The depressed person sees a big discrepancy between what he aspired to in terms of human relations and life goals and what he can achieve in this meagre reality. He cannot solve the conflict. What is available is not acceptable to him, and what would be acceptable he cannot grasp. He experiences the tragic situation of having no choice.

Silvano Arrietty

The psychological rigidity or the foreclosure to the alternative ways of living is especially prevalent in those who live for a dominant other or a dominant goal. We all run the risk of becoming too rigid in our ways. Most people glue themselves a little too tightly to a certain persona or social mask and rely too heavily on things such as looks or other status symbols for their feelings of worth. To avoid the pitfalls of psychological rigidity we should take a page out of the stoic playbook and periodically meditate on the fact that we can and indeed probably will lose some of the things we value most.

> *The object of your love is mortal; it is not one of your possessions; it has been given to you for the present, not inseparably nor forever.*
>
> **Epictetus**

But with that said when we do lose something of great value it is likely that we will experience at least a temporary decent into a sickness of the soul. These periods should not be viewed as wholly without worth for it's often during these times that we see the world and our place in it a little more clearly. As Louis L'Admour states, "There will come a time when you believe everything is finished. That will be the beginning."

> *The intensest light of reason and revelation combined, cannot shed such blazonings upon the deeper truths in man, as will sometimes proceed from his own profoundest gloom. Utter darkness is then his light, and cat-like he distinctly sees all objects through a medium which is mere blindness to common vision.*
>
> **Herman Melville**

To avoid descending too deep into the chasm of mental pain that accompanies depression it should be recognised that there are always alternatives from which we can attain our feelings of self-worth. But to discover such sources an active approach to life must be taken. We must try new things and experiment with new patterns of thought and behaviour. For while a period of mourning can be beneficial following a loss, a deep depression will set in if we stagnate in such a state for too long.

The work of changing indeed the work of living cannot be done on one's behalf by another person... we can learn important lessons from those who have gone before us... But ultimately, each of us faces a unique configuration of challenges and a very personal responsibility for the choices we make in moving onward with our lives. We have only partial information limited understanding and imperfect control. Yet the physical world and our social communities hold us responsible. Such is our shared existential predicament.

Michael Mahoney

But maybe in hindsight we need our depression so it can become a conduit of communication from our soul to relay the messages from our inner core to tell us that something is going drastically wrong within us. Change is drastically needed to put us back on track towards our North Star. Depression is the calling from our authentic nature that the lies and masks we've worn are only ever temporary and the inner spirit is always waiting and wanting to be revealed through us. As Kahlil Gibran said, "Your pain is the breaking of the shell that encloses your understanding."

The pain isn't in our heads, as we've been led to believe. But a disconnection from our authentic selves, the very true nature of who we were as children. We've been socialised to fit into the expectations of the storytellers plot and the attachments to others which we've held onto for so long. The fear of rejection has held us captive, rather than keeping our own true authentic selves alive and free.

A lot of people are projecting their misplaced anger onto those around them. With their built up frustrations and hostilities because of the fairy tales they've once believed don't match their reality. The majority are all wound up and ready to explode at any given moment. Depression is a deep inner sadness from within which has turned in on oneself. It's a dark, heavy cloak worn by a good percentage of people in our culture and it's not hard to be in the firing line. As we're all in the war zone of consumerism and a narrative that doesn't fit in with our natural way of living or being.

A much healthier way to live is to be more in tune with our own inner values and true selves. The way to change our lives around the grief that one feels doesn't have a time line, but it does deny the core of all of us to be ourselves and to experience a life that feels right for us.

As humans we need each other, like when we were out hunting and living in tribes thousands of years ago it's a group effort. Unfortunately loneliness hangs over our culture today like a thick smog, which is making people feel more isolated than ever before. Human instinct is honed for life with the tribe to thrive and be a part of the collective whole.

Depressed people retreat from the world and don't like social interaction creating low self-esteem, pessimism and a narrowing of one's future. If it doesn't looks bright to you, your world will be a lonely, dark and a miserable one. The very lives of many become fruitless and the faulty thoughts that shape their stories. The actions of those that have once believed in a fairy tale, now believe that everything they do becomes overwhelmingly pointless.

The majority live in the waste land of the soul in a world in which force not love, obedience not autonomy, authority not experience, prevail in the ordering of most lives. Were myths and high expectations are enforced and received are consequently unrelated to the actual inward realisations, needs and potentialities of those upon whom they are impressed. So when the fairy tales once believed and inner truths collide, disorientation occurs and the meaning of the narrative vanishes into thin air, as all illusions naturally do.

People surely suspect that attaining material success and power laden status will bring them inner peace. Unfortunately they come to the realisation they've all been tricked by a fairy tale from the storytellers whose aim and mission is to deceive and manipulate. "One of my clients expressed it this way, "I always sought to win whatever the game was, and only now do I realise how much I have been played by the game. I played the game hard and willingly, always thinking I was winning something. But in the end there really was nothing to win, or what I did win really didn't matter." How eloquently his words describe the discoveries of so many of us. While this insight is hardly new, we all have to discover it in our own way and in time along our path before we believe it and if we don't the wound festers without new vision, or without healing.

For many years we've believed and been told from most doctors and the manipulative marketing giants of the antidepressant companies that depression is a chemical imbalance of the serotonin levels in the brain. But this is only true for a small percentage of people with a set of genes. Thirty-seven percent of people will inherit these genes and they only become activated by their environment, circumstance, a stressful event or childhood trauma.

The brain recognises a pained felt response from all the terrible outside circumstances we've become subjected to. When the brain feels like this, it goes into a state of survival mode. The brain and body feel like they're under constant and perpetual attack and the nervous system goes into overdrive. This state creates a division between the two and they no longer work together, creating a state of imbalance. The body is no longer in homeostasis, creating a toxic environment for the body to function in. Inner tension, and stress develops and if this persists over a long period of time, dis-ease creeps in.

It's now been proven scientifically our brains are always changing depending on our outside personal circumstances of distress, thoughts and environment and how we are living our lives daily. This is called neuroplasticity, were the brain restructures itself based on its own experiences. Our brains are constantly changing to meet our needs, pruning synapses we don't use and growing synapses we do use. The longer you have certain negative thoughts and ruminate on those cognitions and experiences, the stronger the neural pathways will be. The stronger a particular thought or action the stronger the neural pathway in the brain. Just like a groove on a record it gets deeper entrenched into the psyche. Before we get a chance to be rational and put circumstances into perspective, the brain goes into fight mode and this causes great distress and despair to the person who entertains such thoughts, feelings and behaviours.

The world we live in is powerful and tragically geared to causing a high background level of anxiety and widespread level of depression. I'm going to share with you, The School of Life, which is a global organisation that helps people lead better lives has six particular features of modernity that have this psychologically disturbing effect on us all. At the end of each one there's an action plan, to navigate around these psychological disturbances.

1) MERITOCRACY

Our societies, tell us that everyone is free to make it if they have the talent and energy. The downside of this ostensibly, liberating and beautiful idea is that any perceived lack of success is taken to be not, as in the past an accident or misfortune, but a sure sign of a lack of talent or laziness. If those at the top deserve all their success, then those at the bottom must surely deserve all their failure. A society that thinks of itself as meritocratic turns poverty from a problem to evidence of damnation and those who have failed from unfortunates to losers. The cure is a strong culturally endorsed belief in two big ideas: luck which says success doesn't just depend on talent and effort; and tragedy which says good people can fail and deserve compassion rather than contempt.

2) INDIVIDUALISM

An individualistic society preaches that the individual and their achievements are everything and that everyone is capable of a special destiny. It is not the community that matters; the group is for no-hopers to be regarded as a curse. The result is that the very thing that most of us will end up being, statistically speaking which is associated with freakish failure and shame. The cure is a cult of the good ordinary life and the proper appreciation of the pleasures and quiet heroism of the everyday.

3) SECULARISM

Secular societies cease to believe in anything that is bigger than or beyond themselves. Religions used to perform the useful service of keeping our petty ways and status battles in perspective. But now there's nothing to see or relativise humans, whose triumphs and mishaps end up feeling like a be all and end all. A cure would involve regularly using sources of transcendence. To generate a benign, relativising perspective on personal sorrows: music, sounds of the rainforest, the stars at night, the vast spaces of the desert or the ocean would humble us all in consoling ways.

4) ROMANTICISM

The philosophy of romanticism tells us that each of us has one very special person out there who can make us completely happy. Yet mostly we have to settle for moderately bearable relationships with someone who is very nice in a few ways and pretty difficult in many others. It feels like a disaster in comparison with our original huge hopes. The cure is to realise that we didn't get it wrong: we were just encouraged to believe in a very improbable dream. Which is the message of this book. Instead we should build up our ambitions around, accepting ourselves, friendship and nonsexual love.

5) THE MEDIA

The media has immense prestige and a huge place in our lives but routinely directs our attention to things that scare, worry, panic, and enrage us while denying us agency or any chance for effective personal action. It typically depends on human nature, without a balancing exposure to normal good intentions, responsibilities and decency at its worst it edges us towards mob justice. The cure would be news that concentrated on presenting solutions rather than generating outrage that was alive to systematic problems rather than gleefully emphasising scapegoats and emblematic monsters. So that would regularly remind us that the news we most need to focus on comes from our own lives and experiences.

6) PERFECTIBILITY

Modern societies stress that it is within our remit to be profoundly content, sane and accomplished. As a result we end up loathing ourselves, feeling weak and sensing we've wasted our lives. A cure would be a culture that endlessly promotes the idea that perfection is not within our grasp. That being mentally slighted and at points very unwell is an inescapable part of the human condition. More importantly what we need are good friends with whom we can sit and honestly discuss our real fears and vulnerabilities. The forces of psychological distress in our world are currently much wealthier and more active than the needed cures. We deserve tender pity for the price we have to pay for being born in modern times. But more hopefully cures are now open to us individually and collectively if we only recognise with sufficient clarity the sources of our true anxieties and sorrows.

"Well, what does 'free' mean? Free means being, for one thing. It means being able to outgrow that knee jerk reflection of what your human society around you wants you to think and so 'free' means thinking for yourself and not accepting every piece of information or opinion heedlessly."

Gary Snyder

Stories are in, under, and behind everything. Our identities, our beliefs, our friendships and families, our societies, and so on. Stories have a way of not only entertaining, but training us. They can be incredible, powerful and beautiful devices that form and assist our perception and understanding of the world. As Fyodor Dostoyevsky said, "How can you live and have no story to tell."

However, according to twentieth century American author Kurt Vonnegut. Stories rarely tell the truth. Things happen to us in our lives and who and what we can change. But our story maintains its ambiguity around whether or not the events that occur are conclusively good or bad. We really never know until later on. As Arthur Schopenhauer said, "Life can only be understood backwards, but must be lived forwards." We are so seldom told the truth. We don't know enough about life to know what the good news is and what the bad news is and we always just respond to that. It's better not to live in a state of extremes, always up or down from one moment to the next but find a happy median, in the middle somewhere. But unfortunately the majority can never find ultimate peace or freedom from the uncertainty between good and ill fortune. Let me now introduce you to the Chinese farmer.

THE CHINESE FARMER

Once upon a time there was a Chinese farmer who lost a horse, it ran away. And all the neighbours came around that evening and said, "That's too bad," and he said, "Maybe." The next day the horse came back and brought several wild horses with it. And all the neighbours came around, "Well that's great isn't it," they said. And he said, "Maybe." The next day the son was attempting to tame one of these horses and was riding it, and broke his leg. All the neighbours came around in the evening and said, "Well that's too bad," the farmer said, "Maybe." The next day the conscription officers looking for people to join the army and they rejected his son because he had a broken leg. And all the neighbours came around in the evening and said, "Isn't that wonderful," and he said, "Maybe."

As Alan Watts said, "The process of nature is an integrated process of immense complexity. And it's pretty impossible to tell if anything that happens in life is good or bad. Because you never know what will be the consequences of the misfortune, or you'll never know the consequences of good fortune."

We as souls living life are a part of a never ending cycle of change, through conflict and resolution. Things only come to an end when things run their natural course, but try as we may, we fight our whole lives to stay away from this moment. Our lives don't end, we just find meaning through our heartfelt experiences within the endless cycle of change and living one's life. Change in our lives are just not for the sake of some conclusion or ultimate peace but a continuation for the sake that our lives are perpetual, to keep life alive and interesting.

As Joseph Campbell said, "What I think is that of a good life is one hero journey after another. Over and over again you are called to the realm of adventure, you are called to new horizons. Each time there is the same problem: Do I dare? And then if you do dare, the dangers are there and the help also and the fulfilment or the fiasco."

Some stories can help us see and understand various micro-moments and aspects of life. They help us better connect and share ideas, lessons and meaning. They can be beautiful, essential devices of a conscious life. Some stories don't always have to be real or accurately representative of life to be helpful and important. But the truth is we often see life, the same way that our favourite stories do. It is no coincidence that most good stories share the same basic structure, ingredients, and shapes.

They're a reflection of how we often like to think and how we often want the world to be. However, when we assume and distortedly believe that our entire life can fit neatly into the templates of the storytellers. We are so often inclined to believe and try to model our life after, when we expect or pretend to always know what good or bad fortune is. We create an expectation in every decision, action and event that carries so much pressure. We are likely to fear any decision or put blindly in the wrong direction for our own good.

This unknown can be rather terrifying but, the fear is only intensified to an unnecessary immobile state of paralysis when we maintain the assumption that there can never be a perfect, right decision in anything that will lead to an ultimate noble resolution of everything. So we must forge onwards through our story trying our best to navigate with decency, effort and honesty. Accepting whatever our decisions might cause and whatever events might occur onto us and have an understanding that so long as we are still alive our story will go on and maintain the qualities of all stories: an opportunity for further experiences, adaption and triumph. Even though we can't know what the good or bad news is within the bigger picture. I believe we don't really need to know to be able to look around and know when things are nice amidst it all. To recognise the happy moments in our lives, however big or small and stop and say, "I'm enjoying myself in this moment" We have a culture in which the majority beat themselves up if you're not perfect, it's about time we all let ourselves off the hook and weren't so serious.

> *"Most people are, in the most ordinary sense, very limited. They pass their time, day after day, in idle, passive pursuits, just looking at things, at games, television, whatever. Or they fill the hours talking, mostly about nothing of significance. Of comings and goings, of who is doing what, or the weather, of things forgotten almost as soon as they are mentioned. They have no aspirations for themselves beyond getting through another day doing more or less what they did yesterday. They walk across the stage of life, leaving everything about as it was when they entered, achieving nothing, aspiring to nothing, having never a profound or even original thought. This is what is common, usual, typical, indeed normal. Relatively few rise above such a plodding existence."*
>
> **Richard Taylor**

Some may argue there is nothing wrong with this type of normal existence. Modern life can be high-paced, stressful and with mental health problems on the rise perhaps what is needed is more time spent resting and relaxing. Although too much inactivity rather than promoting mental health, tends to breed unhappiness in a plethora of psychological problems. I've observed that depression, with the majority of my clients, were typically preceded by prolonged periods of passivity. When people don't occupy their days with interesting tasks, challenges and problems to solve they discover that depressive moods wash over them, fog their perceptions and cause them to become pessimistic of the human condition. It's been said, "The idle mind is the devils workshop" and I believe this statement to be true. As Colin Wilson said, "Boredom, passivity, stagnation these are the beginning of mental illness, which propagates itself like scum on a stagnant pond"

I do believe there is merit between passivity and mental illness. So at some stage of our lives we'll be confronted with the following options. We can waste our leisure in idle pursuits and leave our untapped potential untouched and render ourselves prone to mental illness. Or we can strive to spend the majority of our free time creating, exploring, learning, and doing. Challenging our capacities and improving our talents. While the latter entails perseverance, struggle and the sacrifice of short-term pleasures and comfort. The payoff is our mental health and personal growth, towards our individuation.

> *"The mentally healthy individual is he who habitually calls upon fairly deep levels of vital reserves. An individual whose mind is allowed to become dormant, so only the surface is disturbed, begins to suffer from circulation problems. Neurosis is the feeling of being cut off from your own powers."*
>
> **Colin Wilson**

Being able to express oneself in a creative way and to channel one's creativity, is always worth the effort, as it increases our possibility of being able to attain the rare state of worth and pride. This creates a feeling of love for oneself and an acceptance. But all too often, more often than not and in our culture the storytellers have produced more narcissistic people, or an arrogant shield to protect their underlining insecurities and self-hate. As Charles Bukowski said, "Don't fight your demons they have something to teach you. Sit down and drink and chat with your demons, you can learn a lot from them. Talk about the burns on their fingers and the scratches on their ankles, get to know them."

To be truly proud of yourself you must have the kind of love that is justified by the kind of person you are. That is you must cultivate an extraordinary skill in a specific domain and thus attain personal excellence of the kind that sets you apart from others. The idea that some people are superior to others offends the modern taste. Many people have confused equal rights with equal worth. Just because every individual has natural rights and believe should be treated equally before the law doesn't mean that every individual possess the same worth.

For the ancient Greeks, this was self-evident. They recognised that, while most dedicate their life to fitting in with the herd, a relative few cultivate an uncommon virtue or skill, producing a work of exceptional worth. Or proceed upon a path in the pursuit of personal greatness, irrespective of the applause or opinions of others. It's of these people alone, they then can love themselves in a manner not based on false pretences.

Therefore the next time you find yourself with leisure, and the freedom to direct your own activities, rather than reflexively reaching for the remote, engaging in passive activities on the Internet, or socialising about superficial subjects, you should ask yourself if the comfort and pleasure these activities provide is worth the cost. You don't want your personal genius within you to die, but sprout and flourish. Otherwise the compost of meaninglessness and emptiness spreads and germinates into the seeds of pessimism and depression. This can become a sickness of the soul and decrease our sense of self as a human being and individual.

So, you wake up one morning and realise that you're not the person you wanted to be, you're someone else, and wonder how it happened. You look back upon your life, which appears to you as a caterpillar-track of choices you've made, most of which seemed right at the time perhaps even inevitable, but one by one have narrowed your corridor. Now you're twenty-eight or thirty-five or forty-seven or fifty-two or sixty-eight and you find yourself a very particular kind of person with a very particular set of strengths and flaws, a particular worldview and a particular palette of moods and responses.

When you were young, it seemed as if the future was as open as a prairie, that you could roam wherever you wanted, be whoever you decided. We absorb our culture's conception of a fairy tale. A person should be friendly, happy, popular, confident, and comfortable with themselves and strangers. We tell ourselves what a person shouldn't be is me. We compare ourselves to the fantasy model and we come to the conclusion that we're no good, defunct.

Western culture prefers us not to believe were defined or limited. It wants us to buy into the fiction that we can do anything, free and full of bright possibilities. That we're all born with the same suite of potential, abilities, all neutral blank slates as if we all come off the same production line.

This seduces us into accepting the storytellers distorted beliefs, ideals and expectations that tell us, we can do anything we set our minds to. It's a false idea, a game it believes that all contestants who start out have an equal shot at winning. The majority of men and women who simply didn't achieve the desired outcome, obviously didn't want it badly enough, that they just didn't believe.

The storytellers naturally wire us to believe and assume that our minds are like everybody else's. This conspires us into judging others harshly. "If I can do it, why can't they?" "Why don't I look like that?" All of this is compounded further by the fact we tend to radically over estimate our powers of control. Even if we decide to overrule the storytellers and assert that we do have complete free will, it's been shown that we're often more delusional about our choices and are likely to assume a person's failures are due to faults in them, rather than their biology, environment or situation.

Bewitched by our culture, we expect others to be rational and always in control of their behaviour. We respond with disbelief and outrage when they disappoint, but people aren't what we think they are. We're all not constructed from the same precision tooled machine parts. We haven't all been equally perfectly designed to face challenges of our environment. We're lumps of biology, mashed and pounded into shape by mostly chance events.

But this isn't the model of self that our culture keeps showing us. Instead, we're presented with an individual who has totally free will and an ability to become whoever they choose. So we must take responsibility for everything that happens to us, becoming self-obsessed and follow our dreams, this is what the culture glorifies as a kind of story, which it creates and then sells us as its bespoke hero.

Fairy tales are great but unfortunately they're nothing but sandcastles in the air, due to living in our modern day reality. So what you now realise you've turned into is something like your mother, something like your father, but with a new layer on top that makes you feel modern, more switched on, perhaps even a little bit smarter. Now that you look back at it your just a updated version of your parents. This might be a little too far for some of you, but it does suggest that your choices might not be as free as you had felt when you believed the fairy tales from the wonder years. You're under some genetic influence and that your soul is possessed by dead ancestors who are working in conspiracy with the ghosts of your culture, and the storytellers who deliberately set out to trick you into believing your will and life was your own.

One of the most surprising things I've come to realise on this long and startling journey is that storytelling is a form of tribal propaganda. Just as hunter-gatherer ancestors gossiping about selfish and selfless people helped control the tribe, by teaching its members to be selfless heroes, rather than beaten, ostracised villains. So the same mechanisms exert powerful social pressures today.

The stories of our neoliberal tribe insidiously persuade us that there's an ideal form of who we're supposed to be and that defines us. We internalise this story and this hero. We make our tribes story our story. We spread it around, in our own gossip and storytelling, becoming unconsciously complicit in the conspiracy and then we try to become this hero. All too often we fail. When the plots of our lives stall, when they fall severely short of standard expectations and we can't see our way back if not feeling heroic, then dangerous cognitions of hopelessness take up space in our minds.

We decide that we're losers at the game. We feel self-loathing. We might even find ourselves contributing to the already statistics on suicide, self-harm and eating disorders. But what these stories don't tell us is that it's all a lie. None of us are heroes, not really. As Arthur Schopenhauer said, "Man can do what he wills, but he cannot will what he wills."

> "Some people no doubt are born and destined to be common to live out their lives to no significant purpose, but that is relatively rare. Most people have the power to be creative and some have it in God-like degree. But many people perhaps even most are content with the passing pleasures and satisfactions of the animal side of our nature. Indeed, many people will account their lives to be successful if they get through them with only minimum pain, with pleasant divergence from moment to moment and day to day and the general approval of those around them. And this is notwithstanding that they often have within them the ability to do something which perhaps no other human being has ever done. Merely to do what others have done is often the safe and comfortable but to do something truly original and do it well whether it is appreciated by others or not that is what being human is really all about and it is alone what justifies the self-love that is pride.

Richard Taylor

All across the western world depression has risen dramatically. Why is this happening to us? Why is it that with each year that passes more and more of us are finding it harder to get through the day? Ninety percent of my clients were all coming in for the same common reasons. They felt lethargic, worthless and ashamed of not being good enough. Pain is leaking out of every pore of their bodies. These are the physical symptoms, but what actually makes us get to this point in the first place.

It's the belief that what we've been led to be true by the storytellers was something that we couldn't reach or believe anymore. The story told is just a story and doesn't hold up to the light of living. Being enslaved to a fairy tale disconnects everyone from their authenticity and ultimately a story of their own.

There are factors in the way we live. So when you understand them, it opens up a different way of going about a set of solutions that should be offered to everyone, alongside the option of chemical antidepressants. For instance if your lonely you have a higher rate to be depressed, if you go to work and you don't have any control over your job, and if you've just got to do what you're told, you're more likely to become depressed. If you don't spend time in nature and or go for a walk amongst nature, you're more likely to become depressed. One thing that unites a lot of the causes of depression and anxiety is that although we all have physical needs like food, water, shelter, clean air, if you don't have them you'll be in trouble real fast.

So at the same time everyone also needs natural psychological needs as well. You need to feel you belong and to feel your life has meaning and purpose. You need to feel that people see and value you. You need to feel you've got a future that makes sense and the culture that we all live in has a lot of good things going for it, as many things are better than in the past. But we've been getting less and less good at meeting these deep underlying psychological needs.

It's not the only thing that's going on but I truly believe it's the key reason why many of my clients and the forty-five percent of people in the western world who will experience depression at some stage in their lifetime. So it's hard to absorb as we've been told by the storytellers that it's a brain chemical imbalance and all you need to do is increase the serotonin levels in your brain and you'll be good as new, not so. If you're depressed, if you're anxious you're not weak, you're not crazy, you're not just a part in a machine with broken parts. You're a human being with unmet needs.

One of the leading doctors of the United Nations said in their official statement for World Health Day in 2017, "We need to talk less about chemical imbalances and more about the imbalances in the way we live." Drugs do give real relief to some people. But precisely because this problem goes deeper than their biology, the solutions need to go much deeper too.

But one of the main reasons for depression is that we're the loneliest societies in human history. There was a recent study done in America that asked, "Do you feel like you're no longer close to anyone? Thirty-nine percent of people said that described them. In the international measurements of loneliness, Britain and the rest of Europe are just behind the United States.

So why are we here? Why are we alive? One key reason is that our ancestors on the Savannahs of Africa were really good at one thing. They weren't bigger or faster than the animals they took down a lot of the time, but they were much better at banding together into groups and cooperating. This was our superpower of our species that we band together. Just like bees evolved to live in a hive, humans evolved to live in a tribe.

We are the first humans ever to disband our tribes and it's making the majority feel awful. But it doesn't have to be this way. I've seen a lot of my clients coming to see me who are totally depressed most of the time for totally understandable reasons, like loneliness.

So instead of trying to do it all alone and drawing on your own resources as an individual, as this is what's partly got us into this crisis in the first place, it lies on reconnecting with something bigger than yourself.

Just as junk food has taken over our diets and make us physically sick, a kind of junk values, high expectations, unobtainable standards and superficial ideals has taken over our minds and have made us mentally sick.

For thousands of years philosophers have said, "If you think life is all about money, status and showing off, you're going to feel like crap." So the more money you can have to display your way out of sadness and into a good life, the more likely you are to become depressed and anxious. Secondly as a society, we have become much more driven by these beliefs as that's what we've been told by the storytellers.

All throughout our lives, under the weight of advertising, television, Instagram and everything like them, we've all been trained to look for happiness in the wrong places. Just like junk food doesn't meet our nutritional needs and actually makes us feel terrible, junk values and cosmetic ideals don't meet our psychological needs, and they take you away from a good life.

It's amazing how we've all done this when we feel down. We simply medicate ourselves with some kind of show-off, grand external solution, believing it will fill the empty void within us. But when you think about being on your deathbed, you won't be thinking about your status, wealth or objects that you think are an extension of you. Just remember we're all buried in the same size hole and you won't be taking anything materialistic with you, so this will make you realise what's important.

You're more going to think about moments of meaning, love and connection with others in your life. Now when we become aware of our actions and the reasons why we fill our emptiness up with materialistic junk to feel better about ourselves psychologically, we feel very strange indeed.

So what's it going to take, what's the remedy to become psychologically healthier? What's the antidote for this world wide affliction that will affect close to half of the population? Which is now being recognised as the most debilitating illness globally. It's all about finding a connection back to ourselves and what really matters most to you.

You must tie yourself more deeply to collectives, friends, family and a cause much larger than yourself. Changing your environment, so you're not surrounded by triggers that get you thinking about things that depress you. Such as cutting back on social media, television, the news and advertising. Spending more time face to face with people who have a similar outlook to life as you do. People that empower and challenge you but won't hinder or disempower your growth as an individual. Pursuing causes that really matter to you, instead of asking what's wrong with me? Ask what matters to you and do that. Spending more time with your kids, nieces and nephews. Spend more time in the garden, volunteering, channelling your creativity, writing and having family conversations.

These are the intrinsic motivations that move you, work on intrinsic goals that make you feel better inside and which help others and the community that you live in. It's not about appearances, it's about what's inside a person, their inner qualities. Love, compassion, empathy and forming close connections with others and family. Getting connected with others restores human nature. We don't need to be drugged but we do need a sense of belonging, being needed and to be valued by others and ourselves.

Meaningless work makes us depressed. Eighty-seven percent of people dislike their jobs. It's not the responsibility that disconnects people from their work, but enduring monotonous, soul destroying work does. If it's deadening you and you're shattered after work, then people desensitise themselves in front of the television, because this reduces our desire to make a difference and the reality of one's life. We all have a choice to change our lives and what we'd like to do so we all can feel equal and have a feeling of respect, status or keep on feeling humiliated. So doing work that makes you feel more autonomous, less controlled and doing something that matters which you believe has contributed to making a difference for others and your community is of real lasting benefit.

Happiness is really feeling like you've impacted another human positively. So you must really ask yourself the question, are you really going to do what you want to do? Are you really going to do something that fulfils you? Or are you just going to stay in your job that doesn't fulfil you or challenge you.

Taking walks in nature has been scientifically proven to lower blood pressure, lowering heart rate and increasing creativity which is five times better for mood and concentration. Walking and exercise also significantly reduce depression and anxiety, giving oneself a strong sense of oneness with others and nature. Being in nature gives you a feeling of awe, it's something larger than yourself, you feel connected to everything around you and you realise you are one more node in this enormous tapestry. Sitting in a park or going for a walk in the woods and reconnecting with the beauty which surrounds you makes you feel insignificant and makes you realise how tiny we are in the universe.

Gardening is proven to be better than antidepressants, so getting out there and enjoying your rose garden or having a little vegetable patch and putting your hands in the soil, is a great grounding exercise. This has not only a benefit psychologically for your mental health, but also a healthy and cleaner way for you to enjoy organic food, and a healthier lifestyle.

Everything in our society is about convenience and we no longer have to leave our homes for anything, technology has given us this opportunity. We can get our groceries delivered, entertainment on our television screens, laptops have become the new board rooms of the western world and unfortunately our smart phones have disconnected us from those that are sitting across from us right now. The majority have lost the skill of how to relate interpersonally. Depression is a disconnection from ourselves and from those we love.

It's amazing how many of us have a roof over our heads, to shelter us from the elements of nature, but within those four walls where love is supposed to exist, most times it doesn't. A lot of people don't have others to love and confide in, to share their concerns, worries and dreams or to truly understand them. And if there's people in the house who have drifted apart because of the realities and responsibilities of living life, non-communication, working long hours and technology are usually the culprits. Dependency isn't love and this creates an inner emptiness, dis-connection, suffering and loneliness. Creating a spiritual homelessness within ourselves and those we once loved.

If you believe this is you, take it upon yourself to seek shelter and open up the windows of direct communication with someone you want to connect with and relate to. Find an understanding of yourself and share everything which is you and each other and you'll no longer be spiritually homeless or lonely and you may just reunite a spark of connection.

Your life will become more enriched, meaningful and happier because you'll be more intrinsically wealthier than those with their big houses and toys which in the end they'll find will never love them back. A house is just a house, bricks and mortar. But a home is the love that is shared through the genuine connections found by talking, listening and loving those who share the same space. It's always better to love and accept yourself with those that you connect with and to know who will love you back and empower you. It's better to always love than to never have taken the risk to love someone with all your heart. As that's what life is all about, love and accepting ourselves and others.

At some level we know this consciously, but in this culture we don't live by it. It's because we live in a machine that is designed to get us to neglect what is important about life. It's better to remember a time in your life when you found meaning and purpose and the most important thing is to dedicate and pursue what you're truly passionate about. It's those experiences in life when time goes by, that you can warp time because you're so engrossed in enjoying yourself.

So what values do you live by and stand for as this can be an amazing remedy from the barrage of depression-generating messages from the storytellers and what we've taken on as our own. The storytellers have trained us to seek happiness in the wrong places and unfortunately not towards more meaning or to be more authentically ourselves.

But why is it so hard for all of us to comprehend? That we have to change our understanding of what depression actually is. There are very real biological contributions to depression, but if we allow the biology to become the whole picture as the majority who take prescribed medication have been lead to believe, your pain doesn't mean anything. It's just a malfunction, it's like a glitch in a computer program or it's just a wiring problem in your brain.

This chapter isn't about hopelessness, on the contrary, what it actually leads us towards is a better way of finding inner peace, fulfilment and becoming whole. The first step is to stop believing in the storytellers propaganda. Once you realise that it's all an act of coercion, that it's your culture trying to turn you into someone you can't really be. You can begin to free yourself from its demands, be yourself and write your story at last.

It's more about coming to a self-acceptance, a quiet understanding and an awareness that the way we are occasionally may cause offence, to ourselves. We try and compensate, and sometimes apologise as well, but also try to attack ourselves for being not perfect. What we've been raised in can't help but become us, to a great extent. We're never going to be able to fully defend ourselves to its demands. But by simply knowing the storytellers high standards and expectations are faulty and not true to our reality. Can be such a deep comfort for all who want to awaken from the spell.

Stopping the war of perfectionism that's happening in your head is just the first step. Once you quit trying to be who you're not, you can make an assessment of the things you're doing with your life. It's crucial to understand our limitations so that you can pursue your goals that are important to you. We need to invest in those projects that bring meaning to us but which are achievable, and if they're not achievable, then you just don't say, "Life's wretched," you think of something else and other ways of bringing meaning and value into your life.

It's just like putting a grizzly bear on an iceberg it becomes miserable. Now release it into the wilderness. The core of who the grizzly bear is hasn't altered in the slightest and yet it's become happy. Its experience of life, but not itself, has transformed. If we want to inch towards happiness, then we should stop trying to live up to the lofty expectations and unreachable standards of our culture and live from our own true core.

Doing the things that matter most to you, the people you're sharing it with and the goals that will challenge you. We should find projects to pursue which are not only meaningful to us, but match our intrinsic values as well. It doesn't have to be your job, it doesn't have to be something grandiosely altruistic, it's just has to be you.

IMPRESSIVE RESULTS USING PSILOCYBIN MUSHROOMS

MY INTRODUCTION

I have always loved listening to Terrence McKenna an American ethnobotanist, mystic, psychonaut, lecturer, author and an advocate for the responsible use of naturally occurring psychedelic plants. I've watched and listened to him on YouTube and have read all of his books. It was Terrence who introduced me to these natural teachers (Psilocybin mushrooms) given to us from mother Gaia. (Planet earth)

Psychedelics is derived from Ancient Greek "Psyche" which means mind or soul, and "Delin" means to show or reveal. So this translates into "mind revealing" or commonly referred as "mind expanding." Psilocybin mushrooms have been used as tools to expand states of consciousness since the dawn of time. They delve further into the subconscious mind to get to a deeper understanding of what one has suppressed. As I wrote about earlier in regards to why depression is a disconnect from the soul. Psilocybin mushrooms reveal what you need to do to reinstate balance, peace and inner harmony. These revelations come in the form of insights, reflections that pop into your consciousness while you're having a trip. Which simple means while you're in an expanded state of consciousness.

LIFTING THE STIGMA

It's not my purpose to promote the use of any legal or illegal substances. But to tell you of my own transformative experience while under the influence of psilocybin mushrooms and to lift the stigma surrounding psilocybin mushrooms. The amazing effects I've had and many others using these amazing fungi which science now believes as well. There's so much potential in both medicine, research and in terms of personal development as they can be used as personal tools, to reclaim your authentic nature, restore balance and heal yourself.

HISTORY

The taking of magic mushrooms has been used for thousands of years in shamanic rituals from all indigenous cultures from around the world. Psilocybin mushrooms have been and continue to be used in indigenous New World cultures in religious, divinatory, or spiritual contexts. They've been depicted in Stone Age rock art in Africa and Europe, but are most famously represented in the Pre-Columbian sculptures and glyphs seen throughout North, Central and South America.

EFFECTS ON DEPRESSION (SICKNESS OF THE SOUL)

Psilocybin mushrooms have amazing and lasting effects for people with depression and anxiety after a single dose and have gone up to 6 months without feeling the symptoms of depression or anxiety. This is a fact and has been scientifically proven which is why there illegal and why pharmaceutical companies don't want you to know. Antidepressants and anxiety tablets effect the same parts of the brain, the serotonin receptors but, instead of binding with them and then exciting the receptor, they regulate the uptake of serotonin. Not like antidepressants that cause toxicity to the tissues, which unlike psilocybin mushrooms none of these pharmaceuticals on the market today can provide long term affects after a single use. That's why there's so much shame around the use of Psilocybin mushrooms and yet they still remain illegal, to this day which is totally ridiculous. There is no evidence of addiction at all with psilocybin mushrooms, unlike antidepressants which are addictive and have worse symptomatic effects and only mask the cause.

HOW DOES IT AFFECT THE BRAIN?

So the adult brain is largely run on automatic software. What that means is you've got about eighty billion neurons in your brain and they exchange signals. They exchange information and process signals for you and this is how you feel, think, and how you memorise. The human experience is dependent on multiple neurons firing together simultaneously, perfectly synchronised in time and no single structure of the brain is more responsible for your human experience. Unfortunately as we age, adults tend to think only in serial neuronal networks.

But when we're born, our brain operates very differently, as children we use a much larger neurological potential and capacity of our brain. We use very different signals, in comparison to when we get older, and that produces some weird effects. As children we question, challenge, query and spontaneously take risks.

DEFAULT MODE NETWORK

The default mode network is your default functioning mode inside your brain. This is largely responsible for your human consciousness and perception as well. So this network is situated in our medial prefrontal cortex. This network is active pretty much all the time. It's active anytime you're not engaged in a particular task. It's active when you are thinking about yourself, when you're engaging in detailed memory, recall and moral reasoning. When you're giving judgements, labels and evaluations to yourself, others and about society. Also whenever you think about the past or future as well. So as you can see we're using this network all the time and, it's active by default. After the ages of six to twelve it gets so reinforced in your brain that you're not really able to think outside of this neurological network. You're not really able to just go ahead and say, "I'm going to avoid that now, and I'm going to use my extra neurological potential." It's just not how it happens, because with age we tend to just fall within these networks, and whether we like it or not it processes signals for us in a specific way. It's because of this network we are the way we are. So this all becomes your actions and behaviours and what you've been told to believe by the storytellers on how you should live and behave or else chaos will follow. This keeps us locked into a set program to live a certain way. Psilocybin mushrooms have been found to have an absolutely profound effect on this network, which literally work like keys that unlock the programming from childhood.

HOW DOES IT WORK?

Psilocin is the active ingredient in psilocybin, and when you consume a psychoactive mushroom, psilocybin breaks down in your stomach, and psilocin is what does the magic. They are serotonin receptor agonists, and what that means is that they don't agonise your receptors or do them harm. What they do is they bind with them, the psilocin molecule is an exact replica of your serotonin molecule, which you produce by yourself. It's an exact replica in nature, it's as if nature was playing copy and paste with it and this is incredible within itself. The way it binds with the receptor is absolutely magnificent because it doesn't do any harm to the receptor, it doesn't cost your tissues anything, and is the exact copy of serotonin.

WHERE ARE THEY FOUND?

Psilocybin mushrooms grow in almost any climate zone. There are over two hundred species of them around the world.

USAGE

They've been used up to six thousand years before Christ came, only in religious and spiritual settings, not recreationally. This is not a recreational substance, it should not be treated as such because the effects in comparison to other recreational substances we are more acquainted with, are completely different. The effects are something that you can't really put into words, as it will come apparent soon enough.

RESEARCH

So I want to focus on two specific researchers to see how psilocin, the magic mushroom, affects the human brain. After we've already established the psilocin molecule binds with the serotonin receptor what actually takes place in the brain is something spectacular.

It was in London where a team of researchers led by professor Nutt, a professor in medicine at the Imperial college of London, administrated psilocybin to adults in a controlled environment and they observed what the effects were. So what happened was that when psilocin met the serotonin receptor, the blood flow to your default mode network which is the area that is constantly responsible for your thoughts of self and others, future, past and overthinking, is always active, almost anytime you are not engaged with anything. They noticed that the blood flow of that area was severely reduced, and the brain was put down in a sort of sedated dream like state. But in 2014 the same team led by an Italian mathematician found that parallel to this decrease in blood flow there was a decrease in neuronal activity, within the default mode network of the subjects. So the neurons of the default mode network, that normally exchange signals to process information for you, are now kind of in a decreased functioning mode, almost deactivated in a way.

So one would ask, "Well what happens to all the information that the default mode network normally processes?" The network would still need to process while you are under the effects of Psilocybin. The brain has got this quality called neuroplasticity which means whenever a signal in your brain, like an emotion or a thought which normally runs down a specific path is not able to for some reason. The default mode network in your brain automatically creates new neural connections. It will create new junctions between neurons, and it will find alternative ways to exchange information. That same information that would normally be processed through alternative ways and alternative paths. But the overall communication of neurons within your brain became spectacularly enhanced as well.

LONG RANGE EFFECTS

The long range effect, as it's called in science, is when areas of the brain are separated from each other which do not normally cooperate to process information were now establishing new connections under the effects when the default mode network was deactivated. There was dramatic temporary reorganisation of the communication and great enhancement in neuronal activity.

The new connections were perfectly synchronised in space and in time. It's almost as if your brain knows how to do this by default, but it's forgotten.

The brain was not even breaking a sweat, it was not troubled by it, but actually resembled a brain under meditation, which is astonishing within itself. When in meditation you affect the same neurological network, which is the default mode network, and it switches down your feelings of self, self-talk and ego. That's when insights and reflections start to reveal and manifest into your conscious waking state. The brain is not troubled by psilocybin at all. So when we switch off all the thoughts about self and evaluations and pondering of the future and the past, your brain kind of unlocks itself. It reoccupies its own neurons that had not been used since you were a child and all this information about what you've suppressed, reveals itself.

THE SUBJECTIVE EFFECTS

The subjective effects of Psychedelics as a trip. The trip is to your subconscious self, a trip to something that you've long lost. These are parts of ourselves that make us uncomfortable with ourselves, whether it be our capacity for evil, our insurgent narcissistic agendas or our most spontaneous, healing, instinctually, grounded selves. And what you're not able to attain, reach and get into while you are awake. This is the job of the psilocybin. The trip is a trip to discovering the deeper workings of you and it's very provoking, enjoyable and interesting. It can be very scary and weird, but life changing and very well eye opening as I have experienced many times before.

SET

Set refers to how you feel in life at the moment, it's your attitude or mindset. Whether you feel loved and accepted, whether you're at peace with yourself, frustrated, upset, anxious or unloved and lonely.

SETTING

Setting refers to your instant environment and the comfort of that. So it is critical for your experience and you should never approach a psychedelic substance lightly. These have been used only in spiritual and religious environments. So they have no place on our recreational table.

INTENTIONS

Setting intentions for your psilocybin trip can be extremely easy or difficult. Intentions are what you hope to get from a trip, what you hope to learn, or why you're taking the mushrooms. They can be simple like, "I'm curious to see what the mushrooms will show me" or more personal like, "I'd like to learn how to forgive my parents."

TRIP SITTERS

Trip sitters can be anyone, especially someone you trust like a close friend, family member or a professional transpersonal therapist. It's good to ask a friend with some psychedelic experience, but not totally necessary. They essentially just need to have the time (at least 6 hours) to come and be a calm, supportive presence that keeps you safe while you enter an altered state of consciousness.

PERCEPTION CHANGES

So in terms of perception changes, people have reported amazing experiences. Colours are perceived and are actually felt during these experiences. You can see them with the eyes, you feel the colours with open or closed eyesight. Vivid imagery, memory recall and a feeling of loss of self, is normal when the default mode network isn't active. All concepts of self are not active and how less important we really are in the universe is realised. As we're so attached to ourselves, loss of concept of time, or time perception has been taken out of the equation. Emotions and feelings can be felt like extreme love, euphoria, connection to everything and one another, acceptance of yourself and at times severe panic attacks, and paranoia. But this depends on the mental state of the person. Psilocybin mushrooms are not to be taken if you're schizophrenic or have bipolar as you may lapse into a psychosis.

AFTER THE TRIP AND THE EFFECTS

Once the trip is over your back to normal but with a different perspective. A deep understanding of yourself and of others, and coming to peace with who you are and what needs to change. With this change comes a different perspective, purpose on your objective reality. Feelings of enlightenment and of awe, transcendence and a different interpretation of how your life now should be lived and your place in the universe.

LONG TERM EFFECTS

Long term affects include your openness to experience and to live more authentically, without judgement of others or yourself. This has been scientifically researched and the results are after 14 months after a single administration. It's due to the psychological experience that you get through digesting the Psilocybin.

OTHER TREATMENTS

Psilocybin mushrooms have been discovered to treat drug and alcohol addiction, smoking and marijuana addiction as well as post-traumatic stress disorder, obsessive compulsive disorder, anxiety and attention deficit hyperactivity disorder.

HOW PSILOCYBIN COMPARES

In London in 2014 the independent scientific committee on drugs, examined the 20 most commonly used recreational substances, was what they discovered in terms of overall harm done to the user and to society, was that LSD and psilocybin mushrooms were in a whole separate category all on their own as the most harmless. The most harmful were alcohol, heroin, cocaine, tobacco and cannabis, which are just incomparable in terms of society and harm done to user.

RESEARCH

Research in 2006, sponsored by the US government, saw forty adults between the ages of forty to forty-five administered a regular dose of psilocybin they discovered one out of five had a bad trip, which is panic or paranoia for a good four to five hours but that the amount of things they learnt about themselves extremely outweighed the negatives. One out of three people reported that this was the most single spiritual significant event of their life and two of three reported that this experience was in the top five of their most significant experiences of all time. It was like a child being born or a death of a family member.

MY TRANSFORMATIVE EXPERIENCE

I had been trying to obtain some Psilocybin mushrooms for quite some time. Researching the benefits and them being referred to as teachers. As one dosage is like one hundred hours of psychological analysis. So I was talking to a good friend of mine and in an uncanny conversation about Terrence McKenna and how I was wanting to have a psychedelic experience. It turns out quite coincidentally, I could acquire some from my friend and so I purchased five grams. However for my first trip I took only three grams to begin with as it's better to start off with a small dose, and increase later as to see how you may be effected. To take five grams is also referred to as a heroic dose, as Terrence McKenna gave meaning to the term heroic dose, because you've got to be a hero to take it. The mushrooms came in a dried powered form concealed in a little plastic envelope. The specific variety I had were called Golden Tops.

A couple of weeks later I was off to a cabin up at Mount Glorious where I go to do my writing for my books, retreat into nature, and get away from the rat race. I thought it would be the appropriate place to have the mushroom experience as it's a beautiful, peaceful environment which relaxes me immensely. I was also in a good place in my life at the time, so that was the set and setting taken care of. As I'm aware it's very important to be in the right frame of mind, as a negative or low mind may manifest as a bad trip. There wasn't any hesitancy with me as I had done my research and was ready for my experience. My intention was to listen to what was to be revealed and put into place what may be needed to bring about inner healing and growth. Although I didn't have a sitter with me during the trip, which was ignorant of me, luckily for me this was an amazing experience. However I suggest you not take that risk that I did and have a sitter with you always.

I took the powered mushrooms as a tea. I boiled the water but waited until the water was warm as I was told if you put the mushrooms into the hot water it lessens the compound effects of the psilocybin. So I emptied the contents into my mug, and stirred the dried mushrooms and drank. Occasionally stirring as not to miss the mushroom residue from the sides of the mug.

After swallowing the remains of my mushroom tea I made myself comfortable on the back veranda of the log cabin. Smelling the pine and eucalyptus trees, with all the local parrots calling out around me was just divine. After about twenty minutes everything started to get a lot brighter and intensify, my experience was beginning. It was like all my senses had been turned up to one hundred on the euphoric scale. All the trees, ferns and flowers surrounding the cabin had energy around them and I could see them breathing. Next moment I went to pick up a glass that was in front of me and I looked at my hand, and it was like I was looking at my hand for the first time. I didn't believe it was my hand, because I believed it didn't belong to me, such an outrageous experience. I had lost my sense of self, physically, I no longer saw my own body as a part of me, it was crazy but it was a truth that I later learnt was a common experience. As I got up to go outside I grabbed a bottle of water, as I wanted to keep hydrated but on the way out the door I went to the toilet and next minute I saw water pouring out of me and I giggled to myself as in this state. I realised I was just energy, but not a physical human being, yet an energetic one. As I washed my hands, I saw my blue eyes and I was astounded by these eyes reflecting back at me in the mirror. My pupils were huge, big and black, rather remarkably as I never have seen them like that before. My walk had changed too like I was walking on air. It was time to trek outside.

As I walked outside the front door I made it to about two steps, I became overwhelmed by the beauty that surrounded me and just cried with pure love for everything. This insight came flashing straight to me, you take the little things for granted, and it's the little things that make everything so important. The insights came to me like an inner knowing and in very small whispers. All of a sudden a couple of king parrots flew right next to me, it was like they knew I could understand them and that my energy was heightened, like it was telepathy, I was in total disbelief and awe at the same time. Then before me was a field of grass and I could see every blade of grass and the colours were so visually vibrant, the green colour was actually emanating off every blade of grass itself. Next to me was a paper bark gum tree and I could see its leaves sucking up carbon dioxide and breathing out oxygen, which was going into my nose and I could feel it going down into my lungs. I felt and witnessed being a part of nature and for the first time realised, I wasn't separate at all from nature but a part of it.

As I walked around I kept on looking at my watch, but time had stopped. Then I got this message time is manmade and it doesn't exist. All the while I'm walking around looking at my watch and arm saying what is that, whose arm is this. I had the giggles like a child because it was how I was feeling so out of the physical and enjoying this crazy, euphoric experience. I looked up into the sky and it was like everything had more vibrancy, depth and texture to the clouds. Everything was awash with colour. Everything was alive.

Then all of a sudden I'm getting all these insights, "Luke your too hard on yourself" "Don't be so structured," "Your family communicate differently to you, learn to understand the way they communicate," "You're a beautiful soul, there's no malice in you" " Why don't you speak to your parents and sister?" "Just call them up and say hello to them and see how they are, forget the past", "Live Today" "Forgive, and forget and inner harmony will be restored to you." In between all of these insights and reflections there were a lot of tears, it was a very cathartic and therapeutic experience to say the least. The chickens were coming home to roost and my understanding that the life I'd been living was a good one, yet at times I had been a slave to material things and my self-importance. I was told that I'm an authentic person who wears his heart on his sleeve, open and honest. I had no ego while having this experience, it had dissolved. At the time during the experience I could comprehend the true nature of life, and myself. Everything is alive and that each and every one of us is connected. Everything and everybody has its role to play and we're all a part of it. Then I walked past my car and I put my hand on it and said, "It's just metal, it's nothing, yet you place so much emphasis on this as an extension of yourself and your identity and it's not." Then I cried some more, as it was like all these feelings of worthlessness and self-pity were leaving my soul and I kept repeating to myself, you're a good soul, and on it went. While drinking lots of water and urinating behind trees to flush the psilocybin out of my system.

The next day I felt so much lighter, like a heavy burden had been lifted, with a deeper understanding of life and myself. My concerns of self-consciousness were no longer with me or any anxiety I was clinging onto. I realised everyone was my equal. I felt really humble and more relaxed than ever. I was grateful for being alive and had learnt to go with the flow. I'm no longer anxious anymore and believe there's a much larger force in control of my life and all I have to do is totally surrender and trust in the higher force of the universe. A few days later I called my parents up after seven years of no contact and to this day I have a very good relationship with them both. Without this experience I believe I wouldn't be talking to them. I did contact my sister as well as we'd been estranged and our relationship is now flourishing. I initiated contact because of an insight I had received telling me, that family bonds are very important and are in need of repair and to let go of wounds from the past. I've done numerous trips since, which have given me more profound insights into my inner life. Psilocybin mushrooms have delivered for me every time, bringing with it healing, spiritual growth and transcendence.

Please remember, it's up to you to educate yourself. It's not my purpose to promote or propagate the use of any substance, it is my purpose to make you curious again and to make you go out there and read what's currently dealt with under the scientific umbrella. I will never tell you to take a substance, but what I firmly believe in is that we as conscious beings on this planet have a genetic obligation to never stop exploring and never stop learning about ourselves.

I believe our lives are a journey along a path to individuation, it's the story of acceptance, being totally honest and authentic with yourself and others. Reality is chaos, chance, injustice, just as our future is illness, bereavement and death. Life is terrifying and most of the time change is out of our control. There's little we can do to manage it but our ego likes to hide this disturbing fact and what we've been led to believe from the storytellers. It leads us to believe we're heroes, captaining the plots of our lives.

It's when we lose the fights of our lives and keep losing that we become stuck and humiliated, broken heroes, enemies of our ever more demanding culture. Then the fairy tale that we've been told starts to fail. It begins to creak and crack and the actual truth of what it is to be human and living the human condition presses in on us. That we see for the first time, reality is stranger than fiction.

All we have ever wanted for the stories of our lives was the illusion of control. But we have none, not really and neither do the people around us who seem so intimidating in their radiant perfection. Ultimately we can all take comfort in the understanding that they're not actually perfect, and none of us ever will be. We're not as we've been promised, 'as Gods'. On the contrary, we're just fallible human beings and we're here on Earth to learn, so why not take the curriculum.

No matter how convincing the storytellers were, it might seem that our perspectives and beliefs come from a personal place of freely willed wisdom. But as you've come to realise we become our culture and the tales that have been planted years ago by those we thought had it all figured out. Sure we're all not clones, of course. We all have different personalities, different identities and past experiences that make up us.

However from what I've learned in private practice and from my own heartfelt experiences is that we're only able to start changing our life when we realise that depression isn't a malfunction. It's a signal and it's telling you something very important and worth listening to. You feel this way for many reasons and it's hard to see in the throes of mental imbalance. It's not a sign of weakness, or madness, but a collective problem caused by what has gone on in our culture and the lies, expectations, ungettable standards we have once believed. So the solution has to be a collective solution as well. We all have to change the culture so we can all become free to change our own lives and stop the repetitive storytelling on the generations that come after us. It's within our control to set the example to not write the scripts for others so we must all take personal responsibility for our own lives and stories.

There's a lot of hard truths that most don't want to look at within their own lives and realise nothing lasts. The relationship you had which was loving and caring, can be now unloving and unsupportive. The job you once loved and enjoyed getting up early and putting all that effort and enthusiasm in for, becomes monotonous and tiresome. The health of your ageing body lets you know you can no longer do the work you used to do, with all of its aches and pains and visits to the doctor.

So start listening to your pain and the chaos that surrounds your life. These signals will awaken you to the very fact that something deep down inside of you is wrong. Something in the way you live. Don't try and suppress your intrinsic values and needs, to a culture that doesn't give two hoots about you. A client asked me the other day, "Luke, what is it going to take for me to make my life better and happier?" I answered, "You must be willing to take part, in your own rescue."

You've got to be willing to go down the rabbit hole and follow the pain down to the very core of your being. You must listen and honour your truth, which is telling you there's something you need to hear. Honour and respect these signals, own it and act out on what's missing in your life. It's only when you walk your own journey, and no longer be blindsided by the storytellers lies and mass hypnosis will you clear a path towards your own authentic journey.

Psychedelics are illegal not because a loving government is concerned that you may jump out of a third story window. Psychedelics are illegal because they dissolve opinion structures and culturally laid down models of behaviour and information processing. They open you up to the possibility that everything you know is wrong.

Terrence Mckenna

If you end up with a boring miserable life because you listened to your mom, your dad, your teacher, your priest, or some guy on the television telling you how to do your shit, then you deserve it.

Frank Zappa

IT'S YOUR JOURNEY

I just want to have a completely adventurous, passionate, weird life.

Jeff Buckley

While our journeys are often associated with stories, we are increasingly seeing it, surrounding us with so many ordinary products being framed as either a gateway to or the unmissable item for exciting journeys, passionate romances and otherwise impactful experiences. It seems we are all called to adventure, and invited to fulfil our own hero's journey.

We see this as well in the way most of us are presenting ourselves on social media. More than ever we now have the freedom to go into the unknown to explore new worlds and to present our experiences as cinematic journeys from the stories we see in films. Finally we all can live the exciting lives that those characters do. We all can be heroes living lives worth telling about, or can we? One thing I do know our lives can be filled with purpose and meaning.

Obviously the growing implications of our growing pursuit for the adventurous life runs deeper than this. As all developments do, there are unintended side effects, new risks and other damaging consequences to be taken into account. Like when does the invitation to a new and exciting thing become the unexpected norm and when thus does potential become pressure. However before we can probably discuss the role and consequences of the now ever-present heroes' journey in our society, we must first understand where it came from.

Today most express the desire for a heroic adventure, but this wasn't always the case. In fact for a long time the hero's journey was only reserved for a privileged few. If we go back to the real stories of old. The adventure was only experienced by selected mythological figures, by primal heroes endowed with cosmic purpose. Often times these heroes were even directly created by the Gods themselves. Half human and half

God who lived their lives for the sole purpose of hero pursuits. Although we now tend to give these heroes more characterisation when we retell their stories. Back then these heroes were far less relatable on a personal level. They embodied certain virtues like courage and strength but given to what end they had an implicit or explicit superhuman nature. A rather narrow heroic destiny in which they almost solely concerned themselves with slaying monsters.

There was a much clearer separation between their adventures and those of our own. It can be even said that a primal hero is specifically destined to exist only in adventurous stories in our ordinary world. Their presence would be awkward and strange, and they probably wouldn't be trusted due to their unreliable nature. We see this separateness in the stories of gunslingers and other lone wolves who have a place in the world of adventure, but not in our own.

The Ancient Greeks believed that people were known by their idols they worshipped. I think it's safe to say that the spirit of heroism has all but vanished from the modern world, and by the off chance a true hero does emerge in the public's view, many respond with envy and fixate on the hero's flaws and weaknesses. As Robert Moore said, "Ours is not an age that wants heroes, ours is an age of envy, in which laziness and self-involvement are the rule. Anyone who tries to shine, who dares to stand above the crowd, is dragged down by his lacklustre and self-appointed peers."

> *In our culture anyway, especially in modern times, the heroic seems too big for us, or we too small for it. Tell a young man that he is entitled to be a hero and he will blush. If everyone honestly admitted his urge to be a hero it would be a devastating release of truth. But the truth for the need for heroism is not easy for anyone to admit. In the more passive masses of mediocre men it is disguised as they humbly follow out the roles that society provides for their heroics and try to earn their promotions within the system allowing themselves to stick out, but ever so little and so safely.*
>
> **Ernest Becker**

Moving back onto medieval times, we witness the rise of the chivalric romance. The stories about knights being the primal hero, venturing into an unknown world to face the dangers that lurk there. The knight was fated for these adventures, they went on quests because of their own choice most often driven by the opportunity to display knightly virtues and when they were done they had an ordinary world to return to. However because knighthood was also a privilege for selected individuals there still was a rather distinct separation between these heroes and most of the people enjoying their stories.

Around the fourteenth century the term adventurer became associated with a different type of heroism that today we become more critical of and that is the rise of colonialism and capitalism. The heroes in these stories were often tradesmen, sailing around the world establishing new trade routes to set up colonies and bring home exotic goods. Unlike the primal heroes and knights these adventurers didn't journey into new worlds to battle dragons and other monsters. They went there to civilise it and to expand their own worlds into uncharted territories and exploit its resources.

In such times as now the heroic adventure has become strongly associated with material gain. While these adventures are reserved for the more wealthy individuals who have the entrepreneurial spirit. The basis of their stories doesn't resonate widely among the general public it still does however have the adventurous tales of the entrepreneur. Even though now the focus has shifted from conquering new worlds to conquering new markets.

The democratisation of the heroic adventure continues in the sixteenth century with the picaresque genre. Unlike the exclusivity of the previous adventures in these stories, for the first time the hero could be anyone. In fact in picaresque stories the hero was typically from a lower social class. Someone who often challenged the rules and institutions of their society. This was the time for heroic deviants, petty criminals and pirates whose behaviour, while bordering on being criminal, was still framed as sympathetic.

Today these are the stories of likeable outlaws, as for the example in Point Break, The Fast and The Furious or Ocean's Eleven. There's one final development that brought us to where we are today, for in the brave stories the adventure was typically open to anyone, it was still something that you had to embark on. The adventure was still driven and reflected by the will and character of a hero.

Around the eighteenth century this changed with stories that featured adventures but no real adventurers. One of the most influential stories of this movement was that of Robinson Crusoe, who was famously stranded and had to survive on the desert island. Crusoe was unlike any other hero in the sense that he himself wasn't adventurous by nature. Instead of seeking out danger and excitement he desired comfort and safety and tried to rebuild his ordinary world around him. As such the main focus of the adventure wasn't directed outwards but inwards. It was with Robinson Crusoes character and stories like these, that the adventure was no longer an explicit journey, but more of an experience. One that can happen to anyone at any place and anytime. The unknown world that the hero ventures into no longer has to be a physical space, but can be the hero's own mind and this eventually led the way to psychological stories.

Stories centred towards the inner journey of the hero is where we are driven to by the hero's own character, emotions and motivations. By traits we all possess and can relate too, and thus our very being became the source for adventure. What I wanted to write about was a very general trend from, adventures as being reserved for incomprehensible, mythological heroes that have been observed from afar. To being directly relatable and open to anyone as this is pretty much where we find ourselves today.

Not that everything we do, everything we experience and everything we feel is seen as adventurous or as worthy of a story, not everyone can experience the adventure, or go on their own hero's journey. What it really means to live life like an adventure, is that adventures and stories are always made up of meaningful elements. They are always constructed in hindsight by a storyteller who uses this vantage point to give order, expectation and significance to disconnected parts until they form a cohesive whole.

This is often done to similar structures which can be assigned to the general format of a transformative heroic journey being a triumphant or a tragic one. As such stories create norms and expect led patterns for how certain things play out and, with the boundary between stories and real life having largely evaporated over time, the heroic adventure now becomes an unrealistic expectation for most.

Stories are increasingly informing with what our own adventures should be like. Of course we don't expect our lives to become adventures in the literal sense that we too will be fighting aliens or becoming pirates. But it's the underlying structures of those norms and expected patterns that we are increasingly projecting onto our own lives.

We see this very simply in the way we talk about ourselves and when we tell others our stories, we essentially become authors of our own lives. And what makes a better story than an adventurous and meaningful one.

Its' fun to go to a party but it's not truly epic until it escalates like in project X or until it ends with a morning after as it does in the

Hangover. It's nice to meet someone and fall in love, but it's not truly romantic like a grand life story like that in the Notebook, or a quirky one that is seen in so many world cinema films.

There's a lot to say about the growing feeling of having to one up each other with ever more exciting tales of adventure. I don't believe we just want to appear more interesting to our friends, but also because these days it's now becoming so much of a norm that it's no longer necessary to have relevant skills when applying for a job or a university. Becoming an artist no longer means just being good at your art, you also need a good story. You need to stand out from everyone else, you are to some extent expected to have experienced adventures.

This is where our consumer culture comes in, as we're constantly bombarded with the necessary items for new adventures. It's not really about the explicit message, but the subliminal one. I know if I get the latest GoPro my life won't suddenly turn into an extreme sports adventure, but I might be able to present it in a slightly more adventurous way than it is now. Even though I already own an older GoPro model, I still can't help but imagine how much sharper, more colourful and therefore more adventurous, I could present my life with this new one. Same goes with expensive fragrances. I know it won't turn my life into that of celebrity presenting it, but wearing one that slightly raises my appeal and confidence, might just give me that extra edge to turn an ordinary night into an adventurous one.

It might seem easy to just brush this all off, to laugh at the commercials trying to get us to buy products we don't really need. But when you take everything together, when every story shows you heroic journeys, when every product promises you adventure, and when everybody around you is presenting their lives as more exciting than they really are, it's hard not to feel like you are falling behind and that you are missing out. That you are not living up to your potential, which I think is what it ultimately comes down to.

By forming a break from the ordinary, the adventure always promises a potential for more. More excitement, more romance, more personal transformation, more fame and fortune, more meaning and more purpose. Even when your life is already pretty good, the adventure will still be there as the voice in the back of your mind is telling you that you can do better, that you can be better, you are meant for more than this.

I think that it's fair to assume that we all have dreams, and there are things we want to achieve and adventures that we want to go on. Maybe you want to start a business and become rich and successful. Or perhaps you want to go on a journey of self-discovery and explore exotic places. It's rather possible you just want to find someone to love because you don't like being alone.

When we set out on these adventures, we often subconsciously do so while assuming the norms and expected patterns imposed on us by the storytellers. We see entrepreneurs who came from nothing pulling themselves up by their bootstraps to achieve great financial success and we believe that if we follow their lead, we can do the same. As that's what has been prescribed to us by the storytellers. Yet as we now know the majority of us aren't destined for this and everyone has their own story.

We see people having amazing journeys in foreign countries, and believe that if we just go to the same place, our adventure will be equally meaningful. We see romances unfold into beautiful relationships, and believe that if we just play the act we are guaranteed the same story.

To be clear, it's not that all these things can't happen, it's just that they are not guaranteed to happen. Your business may fail before even taking off, the amazing journey you go on might be disappointing and not at all like you expected, and being a perfect romantic doesn't guarantee a successful romance as the other person might simply not like you back. Especially when it comes to the bigger goals that so many people dream of becoming; the next billionaire, a blockbuster filmmaker, a world famous artist, they're not even remotely likely to happen.

But yet because stories show these adventures as so relatable and so accessible for everyone, a part of us still clings to that secret little voice telling us, "Of course it doesn't happen for most people, but it might happen to me. I'm not like everyone else, my story is different. I am meant to do this." And the thing is, it is hard to argue against this, because again, it is technically not impossible. But this is also kind of the point, we can't know how our lives will turn out.

By believing in the storytellers telling us that we can, we simplify an endless complex reality that does unfold according to those structures. We create the illusion of cosmic purpose, the false belief that there are specific steps that will lead to a pre-determined goal. By assuming these unrealistic expectations, and assuming that our lives unfold according to a simple plot, to a handful of variables, we are bound to set ourselves up for disappointment. As F. Scott Fitzgerald said, "Show me a hero and I will write you a tragedy."

Just imagine how many people dropped out of college to become the next Steve Jobs or Mark Zuckerberg. How many people recklessly moved to Los Angeles to become the next superstar? How many people believe that, as long as they followed the steps of the hero's journey, they would surely make it? How many did it actually pan out the way they envisioned it?

Furthermore, when we reduce reality to the simplified structures of heroic adventures, we also tend to focus only on those elements that are within our control. On things like willpower, discipline, and perseverance, once again all important qualities that are hard to argue against. But what is especially insidious about this focus on individual agency, is that whether or not you will get to live out your hero's journey becomes solely determined by personal responsibility. It reinforces the idea that you are not only expected to have an adventurous life, but also that you yourself have to make it happen every step of the way. A burden that only makes you more vulnerable to the belief that you need to buy and do all these things that just might make the difference between success and failure. Because following this perspective, if you don't succeed, if you don't fulfil your hero's journey, your destiny, it is your fault, it is your failure. But is this really true?

At this point you might see the paradox that arises when we project the adventurous as seen in stories on our own lives. On the one hand, we are all called to adventure, we are all driven to become the heroes of our own hero's journey. But on the other hand, it's also clear that an actual hero's journey is still exclusive, that not everyone gets to have one. Then there's also the issue that heroic stories aren't just made up of heroes, but also have supporting characters, villains and extras. So if everyone is expected to claim the main part of the hero, who gets to play the other parts?

It's either you die a hero or you actually live long enough to see yourself become a villain. What do all these contradictions actually say about chasing an adventurous life? Maybe it is just that everyone can try, but not everyone can succeed? Is that what it means to have democratised the heroic adventure? Do people have to compete with each other for the privilege of a fulfilled hero's journey? And if so does success really just depend on individual determination and willpower? Are there not countless other social, environmental and genetic factors as well?

But doesn't all this just bring us back to the notion of cosmic purpose? That only some people have the right combination of traits? That only some are meant for a heroic destiny, and that everyone else has to settle for a supporting role?

In the hopes of witnessing a rebirth of the heroic, and to push back against the envy ridden who desire to keep us on the same petty level of insignificance, we can satiate our own heroic urge and understand the role of values in the hero's life for above all else is lived in a service of value. As Bob Dylan wrote, "You've got to serve somebody." The question is, "Who or what will you serve?"

We all have to live in the service of something, if we don't we're like a ship without a rudder. In the course of our life we will be pushed and pulled by forces external to us. We can live in service of another person or we can live in the service of an institution or ideology, or we construct a self-chosen value system and live in the service of it. To choose the latter of course means to make a judgment as to what we deem to be worthy of struggling for, and protecting it requires we reflect on the question, "What does the good life consist of for me?" To arrive on an answer we can build on the wisdom of others.

We can look for role models, for inspiration, but ultimately we must select what it is we believe will move us in the direction of a greater life. The things we settle upon become the components of our value system, for example we may choose to value freedom, truth, beauty, friendship, temperance or love. Or maybe a specific pastime or craft. Which are the things we consider most important in life. As Andrew Bernstein stated, "Loyalty in action, regardless of obstacles or challenges, to ones most cherished values this is the essence of moral rectitude and it is the foundation of heroism."

> *Values advance life they never obstruct life or harm it but as fallible creatures we can be misguided as to what we judge to be a value. The drug addict for example believes he values another hit, the alcoholic another drink, the tyrant more power over others, the envious destruction for its own sake. But in such cases the object of desire is harmful to our wellbeing or to that of others. And so it is of no value but an evil that tends towards suffering. And death values can also be corrupted with time. Some things that are valuable at one stage of life. Lose their life promoting quality at another stage. And in doing so constructing our value system we must be critical regarding what we choose for as Socrates noted long ago ignorance is in many cases a greater cause of suffering than evil intentions. Building on this elucidation of the nature and insignificance of values we can grow and integrate this knowledge to better understanding what it means to be a hero.*
>
> **Andrew Bernstein**

For what is at best a story about gracefully accepting defeat, or learning some lesson in humility? Maybe the hero's journey is not so democratised after all. How do you know if you are meant to be the hero of your story, or just a casualty of someone else's?

The historical overview of heroic adventures is heavily biased to a particular type of hero. One that is primarily straight, white and male. As a consequence, women, people of colour and people of different sexual orientations, were often regulated to supporting roles, portrayed as villains or erased altogether. To this day, straight white men often remain the default main hero. We can observe a trend towards better inclusivity and better representation. Is masculinity always a purposeful part of men's heroic journeys? Despite our best efforts, we still, at least for now, seem to be bound by the limitations imposed on us.

But who are heroes? The hero is the individual whose commitment to values and their true authenticity far exceeds that of normality and whose value system serves human well-being on a mass scale. The hero may dedicate his or her life to justice, to ameliorate the effects of human evil to innovation. To enhance standards of living to knowledge, to alleviate suffering or the freedom to combat tyranny and promote social cooperation. As Andrew Bernstein said, "Heroes place mankind on their supportive shoulders and carry human beings into flourishing civilisation."

Contrary to a modern belief, heroism does not involve self-sacrifice. Heroism is not a zero sum game in which the hero serves as a benefactor of mankind, but suffers as a result, rather than remaining committed to the values that move human beings towards greater flourishing. The hero simultaneously advances his or her own life goals and quests for self-realisation.

There is a widespread belief that heroism does not involve self-fulfilment, but its antipode self-sacrifice. Such a belief is false, even pernicious heroes are a subcategory of morally upright people, who don't sacrifice themselves. As a practical point it's an individual who genuinely self-fulfils and that benefits others, not his or her self-sacrifice. As the hero lives in a manner that tends towards self-realisation while promoting the well-being of others.

These people are rare specimens and in possession of some exceptional attributes. Foremost among these attributes is a dauntless commitment to their values. The hero is immune to the intimidation and discouragement that easily derails the unheroic. They face up to the challenge, rather than cowering from them, and if powerful destructive forces cross their path, they respond with great courage and if necessary engages with these forces in an epic battle of David versus Goliath proportions. They may be exhausted but they persevere. There fearful but they face danger courageously. They maybe both exhausted and fearful but they don't quail in the face of the obstacle and or danger. Heroes are undeterred by profoundly intractable problems and or by dangerously potent antagonists. In the face of either or both, they are undaunted. I believe we all have the power within us, to act in the face of adversity and extreme hardship, but importantly be ourselves and script write our own stories.

To grant us the daily choice in favour of heroism we can engage in the practice of hero worship. We need to seek out individuals past or present who displayed a heroic commitment to values similar to ours, and then we can learn the obstacles they faced, the inner demons they battled and the powerful adversaries they fought and defeated in moments of solitude. We can reflect upon their struggles and their victories and allow our emotions to rise into the ethers of inspiration. As Andrew Bernstein said, "A hero worshipper experiences the highest emotions of which man is capable, a sense of the exalted."

Exalted experiences accompanied by strong emotions are deeply imprinted into our brain and so is experiencing the sense of the exalted while contemplating the lives of the heroes. We admire and we fast track our own heroic education in the process, we add to our arsenal a great antidote to suffering. For whenever we are weighed down by the regressive forces within we can choose a particular hero and ask ourselves the following questions;

> *How would this hero respond to an intimidating obstacle in my life? After all even in absence of the epic hero's degrees of prowess, why cannot I respond with the dauntless and devotion to human life that a hero does? Why not indeed? The answer of course is that a hero worshipper can.*
>
> **Andrew Bernstein**

If you really want to become your own hero in your life, you must live in the service of self-chosen values, and in this modern day, to swim against the tide. For we live in an age widespread corruption of values has led the mass of men and women to gravitate towards distractions, coping mechanisms and empty pleasures. If we're going to be one of the few who counters this trend and rejects the sickness of modern day conformity, we must be comfortable with going against the grain of the socially accepted. As C.S. Lewis said, "When the whole world is running towards a cliff, he who is running in the opposite direction appears to have lost his mind."

To help us maintain our moral autonomy we must escape from the demoralising hedonism of our age and move towards a life of heroic proportions. Maybe we can reflect on the wisdom of Arthur Schopenhauer who said, "A happy life is impossible, the highest that man can achieve is a heroic life." Instead in dedicating our life to heroism we are choosing the best life possible, a life that is meaningful, challenging and exciting.

> *"There is nothing outside of yourself that can ever enable you to get better, stronger, richer, quicker, or smarter. Everything is within. Everything exists. Seek nothing outside of yourself."*
>
> **Miyamoto Musashi**

But who is determined to be a hero and who is not? This also becomes problematic on the collective level, on which the norms and expected patterns of heroic adventures and the hero's journey as a whole. This can create the illusion of cosmic purpose based on some common attribute, be it an ethnicity, a nation, a religion or an ideology. Something that gives a group of people an imagined destiny that not only makes them heroic, but also makes everyone else unheroic.

Not everyone has the courage and the inner strength to fight against the culture and walk their own path. In fact it's a small percentage that follow the scripts that the storytellers have laid down before them. There's a structure of statuses, roles, customs and rules for behaviour, designed to serve as a vehicle for earthly heroism. Each script is somewhat unique and most aren't up to the task.

> *Man earns his feelings of worth by following in the lines of authority and power in his particular social group and nation. Each human slave nods to the next, each earns his feelings of worth by doing the unquestioned good, "I only followed orders." It's this phrase that rankles in the breast of modern man.*
>
> **Ernest Becker**

In our culture today, the majority give into the storytellers obsession to accumulate consumer goods, more expensive cars and bigger homes. Not for practicality or enjoyment, but in the naïve hope that they get social status likes and keep up with those trying to believe in the illusion of their own self-importance and keeping up with the Joneses.

> *It is wrong to say that man is a peacock, if we mean thereby to belittle his urge to self-glorification, and make it seem a mere vanity and self-display. The constant harangue that we address to one another, "Notice Me" "Love Me" "Esteem Me" "Value Me" would seem debasing and ignoble. But when we tally the sum of our efforts, the excruciating earnestness of them, the eternal grinding out of the inner newsreel, we can say something really big is going on.*
>
> **Ernest Becker**

Regardless of however long we keep this fairy tale going, we cannot go the way of the sheep or the peacock for too long, without suffering consequences as seen in the last chapter on the sickness of the soul. These heroic scripts rank low on the scale of effectiveness because of our existential crisis for the fear of our own demise. The urge to heroism is too strong to be alleviated with conformity or consumerist values and displays of vanity. So whether one enters one's life around conformity or status obsession and consumerism, such attempts at earthly heroism are doomed to struggle and fail.

> *We disguise our struggle by piling up figures in a bank to reflect our sense of heroic worth. Or by having a little better home in the neighbourhood, a bigger car, brighter children. But underneath throbs the ache of cosmic specialness, no matter how we mask it in concerns of a smaller scope.*
>
> **Ernest Becker**

If there's anything to learn in its most exaggerated form is to understand the phenomenon of modern heroics and how it relates to psychological suffering. We can analyse a category of individuals who suffer most of the deficiencies of modern heroics. Which is unmistakable and extreme, and for this there is no better category for an individual than that of the antihero.

The antihero is the individual who has utterly failed in his attempts at social heroism, finding both the path of the sheep and the peacock too difficult or to absurd to follow. The antihero's problems are exacerbated in that he or she has failed to discover an individualised solution to fill the void, and so the antihero experiences depression, anxiety, self-hate and an inner division.

> *I am a sick man, I am a wicked man. An unattractive man. I believe my liver is diseased, not just wicked, no, I never managed to become anything, neither wicked nor good, neither scoundrel nor an honest man, neither a hero nor an insect. And now I am living out my life in a corner, taunting myself with the spiteful and utterly futile consolation that it is after all impossible for an intelligent man seriously to become anything, and only fools become something.*
>
> **Fyodor Dostoyevsky**

In not only rejecting the socially accepted heroic scripts from the storytellers, but in renouncing the need for heroism altogether, the antihero has no choice but to play the role of victim, which is the flip side of hero in the dark underground and morally corrupted corners of his or her mind. The antihero consoles themselves by blaming someone or something. Anything for their inability to taste the heroism that could validate their degraded self. They convince themselves they have been kicked to the curb by family or peers, alienated by society, oppressed by the economic system and have been burdened with psychological defects. The antiheroic life becomes meaningless and the paths that could redeem them are neglected, as they believe the forces oppressing them are too strong to encounter. As Fyodor Dostoyevsky said in his book, Notes From The Underground, "I know myself that it is not the underground that is better, but something quite different, for which I am thirsting, but which I cannot find! Damn Underground."

Many will look down from a psychological distance upon the figure of the antihero and feel compassion or disgust. But psychological health in life demands we be brutally honest in our self-assessment and towards this end we may do well to recognise that there is at the very least a little of the antihero in each of us.

This at best leads to stereotypes about those outside of the group. But at worst as we've unfortunately seen unfold so many times throughout history, it can lead to dehumanisation, hostility and even death.

In a society where we are all expected to be heroes in our own journey, this causes a lot of angst and ill health. But what's wrong with being anti-heroic, going against what's expected of us by the storytellers that think they can write the script of our lives. There's this social perfectionism for all to be stunningly beautiful, having to have high status with extraordinary wealth and glamorous lifestyles. For maybe being out of sync with status should be the new norm, it would definitely take a lot of pressure off the populace.

The ordinary in life can be special, maybe looking after a simple but beautiful home, cleaning the yard, watching the children, doing things faithfully and without despair, is life's real duty. Have you ever thought that the true heroic life isn't related to glamour, amazing feats of courage or the attainment of status, but doing the modest things that are expected of all of us, is maybe all we actually require to enjoy our lives. Most of life is taken up dealing with things that are routine, ordinary, humble, modest and to be honest a rather touch boring. Our culture should focus on getting us to appreciate the average, the everyday and the ordinary. Your life is special just for the existence of you being here without the added pressure of everyone trying to live up to being a hero. I'll take being the antihero any day of the week, in fact I always have. I'm happy to be a nobody, in a world where most people want to be a somebody.

So what can be taken from all of this? Should we just do away with all heroic adventures? Are we better off believing that they are not meant for us or that they mostly result in hurt, both to ourselves as well as to others? That they are just dreams that only work out for the privileged few? A marketing strategy that exploits our dreams and desires for material gain? We are a battle ground of these two opposing life tendencies that of the hero, and the antihero. So our fate depends on which tendency do we starve the antihero and strengthen the hero.

Can we even imagine ourselves without these stories? For who are we if not the stories we tell about ourselves? The stories that give our lives order and coherence, significance and purpose? Can there be an identity without storytelling? The adventure isn't just a cornerstone of our stories, but also of our perception of the world and of ourselves. There must be better ways of relating to ourselves and to the hero's journey and creating a better balance between stories and reality.

The meaning of life is just to be alive. It is so plain and obvious and so simple. And yet, everybody rushes around in a great panic as if it were necessary to achieve something beyond themselves.

Alan Watts

OUR STORIES

Your life is your life. Know it while you have it. You are marvellous. The Gods wait to delight in you.

Charles Bukowski

Who are we without storytelling? This is the question we all must ask about our lives if we want to make sense of who we truly are. What's our true identity and what is it that we must do to create a life for ourselves and give it true meaning and purpose? The storytellers speak of their fairy tales to fabricate unrealistic societal expectations and standards for the course of our journey. They give us false hopes to live life to a particular ploy and to split and divide the path that we walk. Our stories have been written by the hands of the storytellers and it's not before too long we realise that these stories are full of fictitious concepts and faulty templates creating mass hallucinations and immense pressure.

Our lives are about self-discovery and living a fully realised life. We all have a narrative within us, but to heed the calling we have to be bold and courageous enough to venture out far enough past the comforts of our familiar surroundings. Our reward can be a deep inner transformation, but to get to the end we all have to go through different experiences, some good and some terrifying, but in the end they become our stories. All of our stories have four main stages or cycles that we all must go through to create a new life. But it's all a part of a much larger plan that will enable us to become who we are.

But to live our own truth, without it being manipulated or orchestrated from the storytellers, we all have to go through these stages to live out our best life and become self-reliant. The four stages we all must go through are separation, ordeal, descent and return.

Everyone on the planet must go through these stages to become an individuated human being. The stories we've been told when we are younger, became a template for our own lives, but not the authentic journey one was supposed to take. As expected the journey is totally different to the journey experienced. It leaves our lives feeling manufactured like we've all been created off the same assembly line. Life becomes somewhat twisted because of this and a pressure for all of us to compete with each other to live up to a more exciting life.

The values of the system are awash with extrinsic and shallow motivations creating surface dwelling lifestyles. We try and live up to the standard which is foreign to our genetic makeup. Creating strangers to oneself, a sort of alienation to our authentic nature. Leaving us feel foreign and out of touch with our true natures. We try to keep up with the absurdity that surrounds us, playing a facade and keeping up with appearances and how we all must fall into line with what's expected of us. Creating strangers to ourselves and to those that love us.

When we are young we are fully persuaded that we are in charge of our lives, and plunging toward our appointed destiny. We cannot afford to have too many doubts; therefore, forward always! Concomitantly, we grow identified with our roles—as partner, parent, and provider. Later, we may question why, if we have served those roles faithfully, they may not have reciprocally served us? Or we may gain enough strength, or feel desperate enough, to question, to look back and to ask, "Just who am I apart from those roles?" "Who am I apart from my history and my assigned script?" Or we may ask, "Why am I here, really?" Then we are often disconcerted to realise that we do not know the answer to those deeper questions. Frequently, we do not know who we are, what we are doing, or in service to what. Only rarely do we realise that somewhere along the way we lost psychological "permission" to be who we really are.

Most of the time we give away our freedom with others and act in accordance to what's expected. We have to free ourselves from a set of principles that once promised a symbolic victory over death. But all of our distractions and stand in role models never seem to last, they never truly fill the void that lingers underneath. The storytellers offer fairy tales and myths which create illusions and sooner or later they become disappointments. The fairy tales told to us can be easily corrupted by people who intentionally or unintentionally act out of their own self-interests.

Our lives are journeys and can be repeated, shifted, depending on the needs and aspirations of the individual story, and the circumstances and context we put our lives into. Our stories can be just as much an inner voyage into the unconscious mind or to an external adventure, as everything from the outside world, must begin from the inside world first.

The storytellers around us have created a serious disillusionment for many people who believed in the fairy tales that they have been brainwashed into believing. Unfortunately the majority of people have had their lives turn out differently than expected. They didn't achieve the success they were after, or didn't go through the meaningful transformation they wanted or found success, status or the love they so desperately needed.

We all have different perspectives on what a good life should look like, mirroring the ideal of whoever is the strongest person in front of us. But in the end all these different versions become a little pathetic. Each person thinks that he has the perfect formula for triumphing over life's limitations and knows with authority what it means to be special in the eyes of everybody else.

What truly matters is to always reflect and stay critical to safeguard your freedom, moral compass and your individuality for no man is great enough for you to become his personal pawn. Always expand your particular worldview to seek out diverse voices and different perspectives. The questions we all must ask ourselves;

What is seen as truth?
What is seen as a lie?
What is deemed heroic?
What is deemed villainous?
Who needs to be saved?
And who needs to suffer?
Who do I have to be?
And who do I really want to be?

There are a number of cycles that we all go through during our waking state for self-transformation and they usually go in this order.

THE ORDINARY WORLD

This is where we all start from and a lesser version of ourselves. Where we are all programmed and socialised into society's beliefs and extrinsic values. To follow the status quo just like everybody else and we comply, imitate with what the storytellers instruct us to do.

I believe we've been raised to believe in tales which have deceived us from the very get go. I also believe we're better off without these fairy tales that put us on a structured journey and a life not of our own choosing. It's not until these stories can no longer hold up to living in reality that cracks appear under our feet and we fall through the holes of deception which has been carefully manipulated by those we entrusted with the direction of our own lives. Leading us to existential dread at some stage in our lives.

This is what makes us live out our lives which don't become our own. But deep down in our heart of hearts, we have an inner knowing there's more to life. That there's an exciting life and a story for us to create, and not the tedious, and tiresome life we've been led to believe.

We begin to realise that the fairy tales that we were told are much different from our own reality. We become consciously aware that our journeys can be corrupted by groups of people that we've given our sovereignty over to and who use it to forge their own cosmic destiny and take away our innate power to live out our best lives. The storytellers fairy tales aren't to enlighten us, but to control us. They believe they feel entitled to victimise us in the process. Always creating views and biases between the masses, creating heroes out of some, anti-heroes out of others and victims out of most.

The stories once told and the basic structures that try and simplify a complex reality is not even a possibility. The storytelling we've heard isn't the foundation of who we are. Is it not a result of the way we naturally experience the world and therefore maybe even rooted into the large principles of a much wider universe. We must now return to our own experiences of the world and of ourselves.

Let's explore what can be reconstructed out of the deconstructed. Let's see if we can find the essence of who we are without storytelling, not just to see who we are not, but also who we can be.

Just because our lives do not unfold according to the neatly confined and predicted structure of the storytellers expectations, doesn't mean we don't or can't experience our lives adventurously or meaningfully.

The existential philosopher Jean Paul Sartre explores this subject in his famous book Nausea. In which the main character reflects on the adventures he experienced in his life and what it really meant to have experienced them. While he is certain he has gone on adventures, he points out that many of the things considered to be vital parts of these adventures, such as unfamiliar places and mysterious strangers, weren't adventurous in themselves.

CALL TO ADVENTURE

Sooner or later we must all step into chaos, as this is where we all thrive. We don't experience growth and change by staying within our safe zones but outside the confines of our normal reality.

This is the call to adventure and it's a summons that we all must go through. Along the way there are many opportunities and signposts that we encounter as we embark on our new quest for a new life. This search will challenge everything we thought we knew about ourselves, reality and what we've been told.

Typically it's about delving deep down into our fears called the unknown. We all at some point will be summoned to encounter difficult challenges to let go of what we believed by the storytellers. It's totally up to us to accept this call or ignore it. Sadly a lot of people are afraid of the call and live according to others expectations. Preferring psychological enslavement, confining themselves within the walls of their comfort zones, regretting the unlived life. As Vincent Van Gogh said, "Normality is a paved road, it's comfortable to walk, but no flowers grow."

Better the devil you know than better the devil you don't. Most of the time, people refuse the call due to their fears of not feeling good enough to take on the challenge, not worthy enough or fear of appearing foolish among those around them. It's our fears and avoiding all of those neuroses and insecurities that we believe make us not good enough which stop us from facing new challenges, better opportunities and a much more enjoyable life. We usually say it's too risky.

What could have been?
What should have been?
What would have been?

As you may of noticed all of our journeys throughout our lives begin with a desire of wanting a more meaningful and valuable life. This comes as an inner calling, the little voice that whispers to you quietly which can be heard by you alone and comes to you in solitude or when the mind is still.

But to create a new life for yourself you must be willing to take action and be courageous enough to take risks and not let your fears govern you. We all must step up to the plate and give life a go, no one ever changed their lives by watching in the grandstands. You have to be where the action is, out on the field of life, but first and foremost you must take a leap of faith as taking the first step is always the beginning of a new story. The universe always has your back and as Joseph Campbell said, "Follow your bliss and the universe will open doors for you where there were only walls."

To those that want more out of their lives they must S.O.A.R which stands for Stretch Out and Risk. To go to unfamiliar surroundings or places that scare you and put yourself into challenging situations that you've never experienced before. As David Bowie believed, "Swim out just a little bit off the shore line and when you can no longer touch the bottom with your feet, that's where you start."

Foreign countries aren't foreign to the people who live there and what is a stranger to one can be a close acquaintance to another. It's not the content of the story that matters, but it's the form that it takes. We turn events into stories by experiencing them as such.

German sociologist Georg Simmel had a similar analysis and argued that the story, or rather the experience of the story, simply results from the process of familiarising yourself with the unfamiliar. A new place, a new person a new event or activity. As such the story is always too greater or lesser extent, transformative. You engage in something new which then adds, removes or otherwise changes some part of your being.

We must all cross the threshold to go from our old story to create a new one. This is where we will experience a new reality and the beginning of growth and transcendence. It is also the point of no return and were our lives will never be the same again because you want a better story. A more meaningful and enriching life that will test all your skills, abilities and even let you discover parts of yourself you didn't know you had.

By venturing forth into the unknown, we receive new information, which changes our perception on our lives for ever. Some of the ways we find about the depths of ourselves is by quitting our jobs, leaving a dysfunctional, toxic relationship, the death of a loved one or maybe moving to another country.

But with crossing the threshold comes trials, allies and enemies. In this new reality everything is different, new rules, insights and new ways of doing and seeing things. You have to learn to adapt within your new life. Challenges, obstacles and conflicts test every part of our being to see what we're made of. You meet new friends and have new experiences as well as facing new challenges.

But the experience gained is worth the insight found. To be tested is to feel alive, to live on instinct, impulse and to learn to live in the moment as this is where life is lived. You come to realise life is not lived in the past or it can't be found in the future as there illusions of time. You see they don't exist, now is all we have, this moment, and then this moment. From one to the next and this is where we get to use our imagination and design our stories from our experiences and lessons learnt. This is where our lives are lived in the present moment only.

> *The moment is the only reality, the essential reality in intellectual life. The lived moment is the last, blood-warm, immediate, living, the present incarnate, the totality of the real, the only concrete thing. Instead of losing themselves in the past and future, away from the present, the individual finds existence and the absolute only in the moment. Past and future are dark, uncertain abysses, they are endless time, while the moment can be the sublation of time, the present of the eternal.*
>
> **Karl Jaspers**

Another way to look at our stories is a distinct way of perceiving time. When we go through our day to day life, time is somewhat predictable or structured. Office hours, dinner time, night time, we generally have some notion of what we'll be doing during certain hours. Then our story can be a break from this structure, which invokes the uncertainty and excitement of new possible futures.

In this sense a smile from a stranger could suggest the beginning of a love story that will define the rest of your life, or inversely an extreme sports adventure could mean a swift ending to it. Either way to experience an adventure is to perceive time differently. It makes the future feel uncertain, undefined, thereby making the present moment more immediate and urgent.

DECENT INTO THE UNDERWORLD

Ordeals are the biggest tests that we face on our journeys, a crisis, hitting rock bottom, not experiencing that fairy tale. With all the illusions that come with it makes you realise that what you once believed when you were younger actually isn't reality. From here you come to the conclusion that life is a lot more out of your control than you've been led to believe. You finally realise there's a higher force that will create havoc over the best laid plans and intentions. The important insight to all of this is that we're all being tested for the path ahead.

When approaching your inner most fears, you must walk through the fire to get through to the other side. These are the tests that help you shed your old narrative self to become who you are in your own journey. All trials and tribulations represent anything in your life that you haven't dealt with. But you know you must take these tests and struggles to become more **self-**reliant and a much larger version of yourself. To get up in front of a group and do public speaking, to get a divorce, reacquaint yourself with your estranged family member, start a college education at midlife or start that business you've been longing for all these years.

What's stopping you from being who you are and what is it that you really want to do in this life? This is the dragon that guards the treasure metaphorically speaking. It's when you break through to the other side from what you've feared the most, do you start living life with freedom giving you the biggest rewards. Inner strength is required whilst meeting resistance yet having the ability to push through any adversity, producing the depth and substance required to live a more fully realised life.

It's only through this can we be reborn, like the phoenix rising through the ashes. The insights and lessons learned become the fruits of our labours, creating the scripts that appease us. This is the highest point of our stories, everything has been put on the line, and from this moment forth, our lives will never be the same again.

A NEW PURPOSE

The knowledge and insight we receive makes us feel alive. Gaining a new awareness for life and a glimpse into how we want to live out our own stories. We create our lives by being totally honest with ourselves and others whilst walking through this world with a much clearer direction. The inner change and re-connection is found in our unique ability to listen, accept ourselves and acting on our impulses, instincts, realising for the first time we're all a part of a much larger fabric of the universe, and that everything is interconnected.

The ego has been humbled and reconnection with the true self and others has been consummated. You realise we're all in this together, without judgement or segregation, knowing everyone has a role to play everyone you meet, the community and the planet itself.

To find peace, love and acceptance, we all must surrender all past hurts and, to reclaim our own healing which is a part of the realisation we don't have to live up to anyone else's narrative except our own. Healing past traumas and allowing yourself to understand what you've been through reminds you of the innate powers you have within, to begin again on your own terms. We must all conquer our bad habits, behaviours, neuroses, addictions and make the unconscious, conscious. It's only when we transcend our demons will we be transformed. All the lessons we've learned through our journey, we take along with us into our new lives and they become our new stories. We now live more aligned with our true natures, and intrinsic values. Opposed to living the storytellers fairy tales that are more congruent with disempowerment and extrinsic values.

A NEW STORY

An adventure however doesn't truly become an adventure until it's completed and can be recounted as a story. For only then can we definitively distinguish all the hypothetical adventures, all the potential adventures, from the story actually lived. Then can we determine the adventures plot, and how each different experiences are connected to each other, and how events impacted others and became transformative.

As such, no matter how you look at it, our experiences always have two fold significance. First there is the initial experience of something, the strangeness of an unfamiliar event, the excitement of meeting someone new or the pain of failure. Then there's the meaning that those experiences take on as we retell them in a story, which has the power to change how we initially perceived them and the lessons learned.

For example, the once admirable ambition of a partner might be deconstructed as selfish egoism as the relationship falls apart into tragedy. Or the initial failure might become the stepping stone to a more significant victory and give the story a triumphant ending after all. Everything in our lives has a double significance if you're aware enough of it. There's the event itself, and there's the larger meaning of the event.

The only thing is when it comes to the stories of our own lives, we are both author and character. In other words we are telling our stories as we are living them, which makes it pretty difficult to effectively capture our lives into one adventurous journey. As our stories are ongoing for as long as we are able to give shape to them, or to change them, when do the individual experiences of our lives take on their own definitive meaning? When can you say that you have truly experienced a journey of your own?

Even though we can experience life adventurously for that feeling to become an actual adventure. It seems that we ourselves need to transform it into one. But this is easier said than done, because while the potential for adventure is limitless, so it seems to reframe it. Whether were trying to tell the stories of our entire lives, or just a tiny journey within it. How do we give significance to that which is constantly capable of evolving?

Look at how often you believe that we are at the start of a grand adventure, only for it to become something that just happened and then passed without any discernible consequences. Or on the contrary how often have we made life-changing decisions that seemed so minuscule in the moment, that we didn't realise their importance until decades later. Even then can we truly trace those decisions back to their source? Are the choices we make not tied to countless invisible threads? Threads that have been unfolding and spinning around long before we were born?

The same can be asked when it comes to our collective adventures, when does a war begin the moment it is declared? Or is that just a consequence of a story that has already begun much earlier, what is the history of a nation, of the people. Where does our story begin? And just as important, where does it end?

What is often missing from our journeys, as opposed to the fairy tales told by storytellers, is it what Jean-Paul Sartre called perfect moments. Moments that mark definitive resolutions in our stories. Like a grand climatic kiss that is implied to carry the rest of the relationship without further conflict. Or in plot twists, moments in which seemingly unconnected threads are suddenly revealed to be intertwined, in which chaos and confusion are suddenly replaced with order and understanding. Moments in which it all comes together.

In real life large scale conflicts, personal relations and quests for meaning are rarely defined or bookended by singular moments. Especially ones that we experience as such while they are happening. When it comes to historical conflicts, we can define milestones in hindsight, the day of surrender, the signing of a declaration. But for those who have actually lived the story, it's probably hard to pinpoint the exact moment they felt things were back to normal.

Take even our current health crisis, COVID-19. It's unlikely this will be over after one defining victory, after one clearly perceivable moment. Instead more likely to be resolved with a slow, almost inconspicuous return to a state that can be called ordinary.

Looking at our relationships, here too we will surely find important moments, the first kiss, the wedding day and other moments of great personal significance. But again these are almost never truly as definitive as the majority of romantic stories we see in films, however there are some interesting counter examples.

The film before midnight for example shows how a couple, years after finding each other in a dreamlike romance, have to face the reality of what it really means to be in a relationship. In doing so, it comes much closer to what relationships are like in real life. A reality in which nothing can be taken for granted, in which every experienced moment can be redefined or even fall apart.

And what about the reality of plot twists, or moments of grand revelations, we must all realise, everything is more complicated than you think. You only see a tenth of what is true. We may create some understanding of things over time but, what is this really if not just a temporary veil of wisdom over what remains a fundamentally unknowable reality. A brief moment of stillness in what remains an ever-changing story?

So is a formed, fully resolved story then nothing more than an ideal that's forever out of reach? Is this the real difference between the storytellers fables and our own true reality? Are we doomed to a state of perpetual storytelling, of continuous narration without closure? Can nothing we do be set in stone? Or is life dependant on just opportunity and blind luck?

There seems to be an unresolvable conflict between constantly experiencing the potential for our lives and actually being able to resolve one. The easy answer is to search for closure for absoluteness on a larger level. We can say that our stories begin when we are born and after we die. A clear beginning and a clear end. But it's not exactly as simple as that, because even after we die, the entirety of our lives can be put into context within a greater story.

Our stories always begin with our families, our country and all the way through to human civilisation and existence as a whole. This brings us to some larger metaphysical issues, for there is one question we also haven't really addressed. Why do we tell and believe stories according to the templates of the storytellers, which have given us myths to deceive and limit us.

Is it simply because that is how we create meaning, how we give structure to our experiences, or is it because that is how we perceive the structure that is already there? In other words, does it originate within us, or what the storytellers tell us what to believe and expect. Or could it be a much higher force in the universe, that has the final say over everything.

It's a question that leads us into the territory of religion, the belief that there is a grand cosmic story. One that is authored by a higher force or divine being. The existence of such a creator would certainly resolve the difference between the storytellers fairy tales and the reality that we live from hour to hour and day to day. As it would give our lives, our existence the intentionality, structure and definitiveness of the path that we must walk here, to create unique stories of our own.

It would give us something to live for as our lives become purposeful journeys from and towards this great creator. We all must follow our bliss, "If you follow your bliss you put yourself on a kind of a track that has been there all the while, waiting for you, and the life that you ought to be living is the one you are living," said Joseph Campbell.

There is a belief someone or something has laid out a path for us, one that we need only put ourselves onto for a meaningful life. It's a solution that's worked well for many people and still does. We all must take a leap of blind faith, hold our nose and jump, so to speak. We all must create our own roadshows and live our own lives naturally and authentically, and not to take the one that's been orchestrated from the start. It's your life, your story, maybe now is a good time to make it your own and no longer leaving it in the hands of the cultural engineers.

If there's a cosmic plot, or the tracks have already been laid out, a lot of people don't know where they fit in. They've lost the instinct and impulse to live life on their own terms. You can try to follow your bliss, listening to what your heart asks of you, to be bold, courageous and emerge through the unknown. Do you want to die feeling that your life was a mere collection of moments, or a contract set out for you, or a grand mission to help you evolve and transcend your consciousness into a highly evolved soul. This is something you have to decide to make your life, your story, more enjoyable and meaningful.

The way to our liberation, is to grow up and live our true authentic life. For most it is soul destroying and disorientating to try and live a life from what we've been told by the storytellers. To fit our experiences into clear and cohesive stories, so too is the opposite.

If we assume our lives are to be without any kind of structure, what is left but pointlessness? But even if that were the case, we would still act in defiance of that fate, we still naturally create patterns, constructions and storylines. It's why today we are roughly the same person as the day before and the day before that and so on.

It's why we can't connect with others and get a sense of who they are. There seems to be an essence within us that simply refuses nihilism, and that should mean something too. It is therefore that Jean Paul Sartre proposed a sort of middle ground, between the nihilism of a life without the structure of stories, and the frustration of a life that's too restricted by them. Basically we should let go of the templates of the storytellers, ideas of coherence or predetermined structures, in favour of creativity.

We all should take our stories into our own hands, and really become our own authors. We've discussed how the storytellers can put pressure on the way we should live our lives. We base so much of our identities on collected ideas of what it means to be someone. What it means to be a man, a woman, to be strong, to be weak, to be attractive, to be ugly, to be adventurous or to be boring, and in doing so we create boundaries to maintain consistency.

We start acting accordingly to that particular somebody we've cultivated ourselves to be, and we can become afraid to act out of character, both in the eyes of others, as well to ourselves. If we truly become the authors of our own stories, the journey we take could mean we can try and be someone new, to become who we would otherwise never dare to be, to break away from the patterns and norms that kept us in place, that keep us small. As for why, the existential philosopher Albert Camus argued that, "Life is inherently absurd."

As we can see life is full of conflicts, limitations and contradictions. But there's also a freedom within us. Although it's not the kind of freedom that allows us to transcend the absurdity of existence, it is one that allows us to shape our experience of it. It is the part of us that realises we will never truly understand our cosmic purpose.

But it is also the part that then sees a sunset, or a smile, a tiny glimpse of something beautiful and feels that it's not. It's however not a matter of rationality or logic, it's something deeper, perhaps this is what we all feel during moments of our lives, bliss. It's the part of us that doesn't just want to exist, it wants us to live. It's the part that tells us that if I have to create my own meaning, I'm going to create as much of it as I can. If I have to tell my own story I'm going to fill it with beauty. It's the part of us that wants to savour every moment, be it exciting and adventurous, or quiet and mundane, to experience life with passion and intensity. The part that wants us, as Albert Camus put it, "To live to the point of tears."

So we've lived the first half our lives in service to an essentially social agenda, namely, the task of developing sufficient ego strength to leave parents, journey into the world, commit to obligations, partner up, serve citizenship roles, to follow the script of the storytellers fairy tales.

Admittedly, after one has laboured and sacrificed to achieve one's small purchase on security—one's home, family, identity, retirement—why would one risk losing it? It is easy to prattle on about the journey, but in the world of daily struggle and achievement, why should one throw these modest securities away? This practical objection makes perfect sense, but for one thing: Our psyche, our soul, wants something more of us, through us, and won't stop insisting. To change our stories, we must change our lives. To have an interesting story they must become meaningful and valuable to us, to have a happy ending.

Fate is what is given to us, destiny is what we are summoned to become. To live a life which is important to us, we must ask and answer for ourselves, uniquely, separately, in the end what matters most. When we resist the many deaths asked of us, we resist the summons into a larger life. When we resist engaging our fears in service to growth, we abrogate the will of the Gods. The poet Rainer Maria Rilke said it best when he asserted that, "Our task is to be defeated by ever-larger things." While the youthful ego can scarcely countenance defeat, the mature second-half-of-life person knows that life is a series of continuing defeats, especially for the delusions of ego sovereignty. To be defeated by ever-larger things is indeed our task, for that means that we are growing, growing, growing.

Just a century ago, the average age of mortality was roughly forty-seven, meaning many of the readers of this book statistically, would not be here, including the author. In addition to that era, social-role expectations, particularly gender constructs, were so compelling, so normative, that most people pretty much had their script laid out for them. To survive within such scripts was one thing, but to depart from those consensual definitions of identity was usually worse—to experience exile. When we ask what value we serve in the second half of life, perhaps having contributed already to the commonwealth, or having helped reproduce the species, we suspect that we are not just here to kill time, hang out, pay taxes, receive benefits and then die. As Quintus Sextius said, "It is not death but a bad life which destroys the soul."

Perhaps this is why we turn to stories, to help give shape to our own, to enrich them. To deepen our capacity to experience the beauty around us. To give us courage and strength, to prepare for the hardship, the suffering and loss. After all that's the only journey that's shared between all of us. The struggle that we all have in common, an effort that is nothing short of heroic.

As much as our journey has come to be seen as an individualistic concept, a way to shape and transform our own lives, I think that in the end what it really does or should do is connect us to each other. To make us compassionate, patient and supportive towards our fellow human beings following the same journey towards a particular purpose. In the end if you have friends, you're not a failure, and what better way is there to become close to someone, if not to open yourself up without fear or anxiety and in doing so to invite them to do the same.

If we let go of all the ideas of who we should be, and instead focus on who we can be, and who we want to be, it can be truly be a wonderful life. I believe we must all embrace ourselves as storytellers, and let go of the structures that demand coherence which limit our creativity. What we would be left with is freedom, for ourselves and for others. Freedom to break free, freedom to be.

Why are we worn out? Why do we, who start out so passionate, brave, noble, believing, become totally bankrupt by the age of thirty-five.

Anton Chekov

HALFWAY

Do not be satisfied with stories that come before you, unfold your own myth.

Rumi

The wishful thinking of childhood and the heroic thinking that we believe we can or be anything created by the storytellers throughout our first half of our lives is linked to our confusion, disappointment and the amount of energy we invest in those fairy tales.

Our childhoods are characterised by fairy tale thinking. Were picked off the tree far too early, marinated with many poisons keeping our true identities repressed. The objective outer world, inner world and wishful world are often confused. Wishes seem possibilities, even probabilities, they represent the narcissism of the child who wants to believe he or she is the centre of the cosmos. Such thinking is inflated and full of delusions, but in a child it is entirely healthy and wonderful. "I'm going to be a princess." "I'm going to be a rock star." "I'm going to be an astronaut." Can you recall your magical wishes of childhood and what life did to them? Most of all the fairy tale thinking that the child assumes, "I am mortal. I am not only going to be rich and famous, I am going to be sheltered from death and decline." This kind of thinking prevails until about the age of eighteen, though battered around the edges. The illusion of superiority, of specialness, takes some hard knocks when even other kids aren't impressed.

Through the pain and confusion of adolescence, the fairy tale thinking of the child suffers some rough wear. Yet the untested ego persists and exhibits what I've described earlier as heroic thinking, characterised by greater realism, but still with the considerable capacity for hope, for projection of the unknown through fantasies of grandeur and accomplishment. One may look at the sorry remains of a parents marriage and conclude, "I know better than they and will choose wisely." One may still expect to be a CEO of a large company, become a New York Times bestselling author, or to be the world's best parents.

Heroic thinking can be useful, for we don't suspect the trials and disappointments ahead, otherwise who would set off into adulthood. When asked about life and its reality I will always give the truth if asked. Although I look into those eager eyes and hopeful faces before me, I say to myself, "In a few years you'll hate your job, your marriage will be in peril, your kids will give you the shits, you may very well experience so much pain and confusion about your life that you may see a counsellor or even write a book about it as I have. Enabling others to live more accordingly, to what matters most to them."

Heroic thinking, with its hopes and projections barely tempered by the world's ways, helps the young leave home and dive, as they must do into life. But it's only a matter of time, as it must, we fail and begin anew all blundering toward an appointment with what awaits us.

One is at halfway when the fairy tale thinking of childhood and the heroic thinking of adolescence are no longer congruent with the life one has experienced. Those who have reached their mid-thirties and beyond have suffered an ample measure of disappointment and heartache to surpass even the shattered crushes of adolescence. Anyone in midlife has witnessed the collapsing of projections, hopes, expectations and has experienced the limitations of talent, intelligence and often courage itself.

"The Gods have two ways of dealing harshly with us, the first is to deny us our dreams, and the second is to grant them," said Oscar Wilde. If you've accomplished your dreams, you ask yourself, "Is this it? Is this what I've tried so hard to reach?" And if you've failed to realise them, and it tends to be around halfway that such discoveries are made, you have to face what the existential psychologist James Bugental has called "The Nevers" I guess that I'm never going to be head of the firm, never going to have children of my own, never going to be a famous writer, never going to be rich, never going to get married." For many this is the time of coming to terms with the recognition that they have been chasing a carrot on a stick. As Wolfgang Von Goethe said, "Whoever in middle age, attempts to realise the wishes and hopes of his early youth invariably deceived himself. Each ten years of a person's life has its own fortunes, hopes, and its own desires."

Life has its own way of dissolving myths once believed and one must, amid the disappointment and desolation, begin to take responsibility for one's own meaning. There is no one out there to save us, to take care of us, and to heal our own dissatisfactions. But there's a real fine person within, one we barely know, ready and willing to be our constant companion. Only when we've acknowledged the deflation of hopes and expectations of childhood, and accepted direct responsibility for finding meaning for oneself, can the appointment of our real lives begin.

As we travel through the middle part of our journeys, the unfinished business of our first half of our lives becomes painfully apparent. For example becoming divorced, one may come face to face with the tacit dependency that the relationship concealed. One may realise that one had projected the parent complex onto the spouse, and comes to the conclusion that one has no work skills or confidence. Then the chickens come home to roost, creating resentment and the desire to blame someone.

But for this new beginning to take place, the capacity for growth depends on one's ability to become self-aware and take personal responsibility. If we forever see our lives as caused by others then no change will arise, and if you're deficient in courage, no revision can occur. So we must find a new way to be productive with our energy. This simply doesn't just mean, holding down a job, but it means feeling challenged by doing something that will create meaning and fulfilment for the second half of your life. Giving you a sense of playing your part as a citizen in the outer world. Sure we all want to hide away from this mad house and shun away in a quiet room, as it can be restorative for our souls, but to flee away from our personal identities and our unique experiences and stories is a different matter. We must run towards our destinies, not away.

> *The natural course of life demands that the young person should sacrifice his childhood and his childish dependence on the physical parents, lest he remain caught body and soul in the bonds of unconscious incest. Fear is a challenge and a task because only boldness can deliver from fear. And if risk is not taken, the meaning of life is somehow violated, and the whole future is condemned to a hopeless staleness, to a drab grey lit only will-o-the-wisps.*
>
> **Carl Jung**

Regardless of how well you've played the game of life, with all your trophies of success, your house, cars and title, it's definitely played you a lot better. You've built up your ego, as per the myths of the storytellers to divide, compete and conquer but unfortunately your successfully attained ego identity has been worn away by the time you've hit halfway of your life. The heartbreak of a failed relationship, the disaffection from those who were to support and save us or the loss of enthusiasm for the career ladder. All represent the ego projections and fairy tales once believed, which have now stripped away. Shame, guilt and failure deflate our once feelings of superiority only now to experience confusion, frustration and a loss of self-identity.

INTIMATE RELATIONSHIPS

Romantic love gives one a sense of profound connectedness, new energy, hope and a sense of homecoming. Love at first sight is the most notable experiences that we can enjoy as human beings. Especially in the first half of our lives, falling in love is all a part of the fairy tale. We have our rose coloured glasses on and put our partner up on a pedestal. This person could be a serial killer for all we know, and only he or she is able to sustain that persona for the time being, but behind the mask is an ordinary human being like us and no doubt pretending to be something they're not. But this person is special, "This person is different," we say, or "I've never felt like this before."

As time goes on the couple move in together and life remorselessly wears away the persona, and one is left with the otherness of the other. Who will not and cannot meet the largeness of the persona they've been projecting. It's all been dismantled and worn away, life is great at doing this, so people will conclude at halfway that, "You're not the person I married." Actually they never were, they were always somebody else, a stranger we barely knew then and know only a little better now. A lot of people don't love themselves, or shall I say accept themselves, so they love the other person more. In the end finding themselves in marriages that will never work because it's not what they truly want or who they truly are. We look at the other and we've just fallen in love with the missing parts of ourselves. That sense of connectedness and homecoming felt so good and was the occasion of so much hope, now that loss feels like living in hell.

The truth about intimate relationships is that they can never be any better than our relationships with ourselves. How we relate to ourselves determines not only the choice a partner but the quality of the relationship. It's amazing how many people believe and except their magical other will save them and give them a greater meaning than we would on our own. The fairy tale of the storytellers is the fusion or togetherness, the whimsical notion that through union with the other, the half which I am will be complemented. Together we shall be whole, together we shall be one. Such a natural hope from the person who feels partial and inadequate in the face of immensity of the world, actually serves to impede the development of both. The once romantic relationship ends up with only two half people as the daily abrasion of daily life wears away the hope and love that once existed. Now one experiences a loss of meaning, which is the loss of expectation as predicted onto the other.

For the well-being of oneself and our relationships, we must take responsibility for ourselves, by becoming truly authentic. If we don't the relationship/marriage will stagnate. To have a mature relationship one must be able to say, "No one can give me what

I most deeply want or need. Only I can. But I can celebrate and invest in the relationship for what it does offer." What it usually offers most is companionship, mutual respect and support, and the dialect of opposites. A young person who uses relationships to prop up a shaky hold on oneself, could not meet the challenge to courage and discipline of a mature relationship. Where one wanted confirmation, one must now accept differences. Where one wanted the simple love of sameness, one must learn the difficult task of loving otherness. By relinquishing expectations and placing the emphasis on inner growth, one begins to encounter the immensity of one's own soul. The other helps us expand the possibilities of the soul.

Real relationships then spring from a conscious desire to change the journey with another, to grow nearer the mystery of life through the bridges of conversation, sexuality and compassion. Friedrich Nietzsche once observed that marriage was a conversation, a grand dialogue. If one is not prepared to truly engage in dialogue over the long haul, then one is not prepared for long term intimacy.

Many older couples have long since exhausted their conversation because they have ceased to grow as individuals. When the emphasis is on individual growth, then each will have an interesting partner with whom to converse. To block one's own growth, even in the mistaken interest of the other, is to ensure that one's spouse will be living with an angry and depressed person. To be blocked in one's growth by the other is equally not acceptable.

I recently heard a classic gender role of the inner tapes we all received in early life by the storytellers. Poised at the brink of divorce, a husband and wife blamed each other for what had happened to their lives. The man said he had worked hard to be a success, which meant to advance professionally and support his family. He did this faithfully, but with a growing resentment that he had no life of his own. His anger turned inward, he became depressed and finally he felt he had to leave the marriage or die. His wife responded that she had played her role as stay at home mum and take care of him, the home and their children and had not lived out her professional goals. She too was depressed.

Clearly both were victims. They had been handed the gender role tapes and had played them to the best of their ability. As had their parents who had grown resentful over the twenty years. Each had also been an accomplice in their unhappiness, but what can we expect of a twenty-something year old, than to play out the script given earlier on in life. They had served the fairy tale well, but the institution had not served them. Especially in a society where the majority are still getting hitched, regardless of the statistics revealing over half will end up in the divorce courts. But the compulsory, "Let's get married and live happily ever after," narrative seems practically medieval, and redundant. Whether people stay together or not depends on a mutual commitment to personal growth. The sooner each partner can embrace the necessity of individuation as the most important reason of the relationship, the greater the chance it will last.

When I ask couples to consider being ten years older with nothing changed, then they're usually clearer that something has to move. When one spouse continues to block change, be assured that he or she is still controlled by anxiety and invested in the expectations of the fairy tale. No one has the right to block the development of another, that's a spiritual crime.

When partners can recognise their unhappiness and ask each other frankly for support, there is every possibility that the marriage will be renewed. The partner is then neither rescuer nor enemy, only partner. What I like to do for those in couple therapy is for each partner to see me for individual therapy, to get a better fix on developmental needs, as well as attending sessions together to deal not only with exhausted patterns of the past but hopes and plans for the future. Thus the marriage/partnership could become the container for, change, growth and love.

CONTRACT WITH YOUR GOD/UNIVERSE

One of the most powerful and disruptive shocks to our stories is the faulty belief of the contract with a superior high power or your God. The assumption that if we act correctly, if we are of good heart and good intentions, things will work out. We assume a reciprocity with this higher force, if we do our part this force will comply. In the end we all find out there's no such contract and when we hit halfway, we all become aware of this truth. When one stands amid the rubble of a relationship, career, health, finances then one has not only lost those things but also often a worldview.

Perhaps the greatest shock of all is the erosion of the illusion of ego supremacy. However successful the ego has been developed and how far it has gotten us to a certain point in our lives, it can't hold dominion no longer. The breakdown of our ego really means we're not in control of our lives at all. As Friedrich Nietzsche said, "God is Dead." We have all become so dismayed with this truth that we have come to realise that one is not even able to manage one's life very well. I shudder to think that we're not the masters of our own house. The whole part of having our fairy tales destroyed, apart from the shock, confusion and even panic, is to be humbled, through the halfway point of our lives. To feel more, surrender or let go, rather than try to control.

Yet out of this experience may come new life and meaning. The strength, courage and resilience found in the first half of our lives can be called upon to create a new chapter and an even better story. Life is unsparing in asking us to grow up and take responsibility for our lives. As simplistic as it may sound, growing up is really the inescapable demand after our fairy tales have evaporated into thin air. It means finally confronting one's dependencies, complexes and fears without the mediation of others. It requires us to relinquish blaming others for our lot and to take full responsibility for our physical, emotional and spiritual well-being.

We all, I believe, must make our fears our agenda. Yes it's a formidable prospect, but I know this to be my truth and the lives of many I've counselled. To create meaning in one's life, we all must become courageous enough to fight the hardest battle worth fighting for, which is our authenticity and a life which is congruent to our true nature. We often still have obligations to children, economic reality and the demands of duty. Yet even while the outer world continues to require our efforts, we must take the turn within in order to grow, to change, and find that person who wants to be liberated and set free.

Most of us have been off with the fairies up until now, our egos have been dismantled, along with our hopes, dreams and wishes. The illusion that one knows who one is and who or what is in control, invariably leads to the collision between the persona and the shadow. The persona-shadow dialogue happens after our illusions have evaporated and is necessary to create a balance of the society we live in, and the truth of the individual.

PERSONA

To go along with the plot of our culture, we develop many persona (Latin for "mask"), which is a conscious adaptation of the ego to the conditions of a social life. We develop many roles, which are necessary fictions. We are one with our parents, another with our employer, and with a lover. Although the persona is a necessary interface with the world, we tend to confuse the persona of others with their inner truth and to think that we too are our roles.

Unfortunately being something you're not, and not having your needs met in the end only equates to a breakdown as suggested earlier in the chapter, Sickness of the Soul. When our roles change we experience a loss of self. The persona feigns individuality but fundamentally it's nothing real. It becomes a compromise between the individual and culture. To the degree that we have identified with the persona, our socialised self, so we will suffer anxiety at being pulled away from the outer adaptation to address the reality of the inner. The persona represents a necessary face to present to the outer world and it also protects our inner life. The persona is necessary in dealing with outer reality, but all the while the larger, unexplored psyche is waiting to be acknowledged. To create meaning is a major aspect at midlife in a radical alteration in our relationship to our persona and what it is to have a more authentic life experience.

THE SHADOW

Since the first half of our lives involves the construction, maintenance of the persona and keeping the fairy tales alive, we neglect our inner reality and true nature. Enter the shadow which represents everything that has been suppressed or gone unrecognised. The shadow contains all that is vital yet problematic, anger and sexuality to be sure, but also joy, spontaneity and untapped creative fires. The shadow represents the wounding of one's nature in the interests of the storytellers fairy tales, commonly the collective social values, ideology and cultural norms.

The more we have invested in a particular self-image, the more we have developed a one sided adaptation to reality. The more our sense of security is invested in what we become at midlife, the more the invasions of the shadow are both necessary and disturbing.

Most of us are embarrassed about something we have done. Perhaps we fell in love with someone at work and had a rendezvous, only to find out later it was a big mistake. Or perhaps abused drugs or walked away from those who depended on us. Who has not awakened at four a.m. to find grinning demons at the foot of their bed? All our aberrant actions represent a blind groping for more life, for renewal, though their consequences maybe damaging to ourselves and others. It's our programming that makes us feel shame, guilt and self-loathing. It limits us. Yet you must, regardless of your fears change, grow and transcend. Don't ever feel discouraged for being true to yourself and what will give you a much more rewarding life experience.

The shadow should not be equated with evil, only with life that has been suppressed. As such, the shadow is rich in potential and becoming conscious of it makes us more fully human, more interesting. A willingness to allow our darkest impulses, as well as our suppressed creativity to surface and be acknowledged. Is a step toward their integration and to make one whole.

At halfway we've all managed to repress large portions of our true nature. Negative shadow contents such as rage and lust can be destructive when acted out unconsciously, but when consciously acknowledged and channelled, they can provide new directions and new energy. Anger is another major example, which frequently erupts during the midlife passage because one has been encouraged to suppress it. Anger means to constrict. Virtually all socialisation represents a constriction of the natural impulses, hence a growing accumulation of anger is to be expected. Often it fuels our blind ambitions and drives us to narcotics to dull its intensity, or leads us to abuse of self or others. When acknowledged and channelled, anger can be an enormous stimulus for change. One simply refuses to live not authentically thereafter. With a lifelong investment in the persona, the shadows encounter with anger is troubling, to be sure, but the freedom to feel one's reality is a necessary step towards healing the inner split and achieving balance within the soul.

A conscious appointment with the shadow at halfway is essential, for it will be operating surreptitiously in any case. We must examine what we envy or dislike in others and acknowledge those very things in ourselves. This helps to prevent our blaming or envying others for what we have not done ourselves. Shadow encounters are painful, as one is obliged to acknowledge a continuing catalogue of emotions not normally acceptable to the persona world, such as selfishness, dependency, lust and jealousy. Previously, one could deny such qualities and project them onto others he is vain, she's overly ambitious and so on.

The shadow embodies all the life which has not been allowed expression. It embodies our lost sensitivity, which when denied, breaks through in sentimentality. It represents our creativity, which when abandoned, locks us into ennui and enervation. It embodies our spontaneity, which when suppressed, routines and stultifies our lives. It represents conscious personality which has not yet been utilised, and it's blocking leads to diminished vitality.

But after our fairy tales have been destroyed, usually around midlife, the capacity for self-deception is exhausted. In the morning mirror we see ourselves. While the encounter with one's lesser qualities may be painful, their acknowledgement begins with the withdrawal of their projections onto others, by doing so and by placing the emphasis on inner growth, one begins to encounter the immensity of one's own soul. It takes courage to examine that structure which has carried one's hopes and needs, but courage can heal, restore integrity and bring life after death.

The shadow encourages us to recognise that only a small part of our potential for life has been tapped and that we are often overly smug and overly secure in our ego achievements. It reveals other sources of energy, creativity and personal development. By dialoguing with our shadow we lift enormous projections of animosity or envy off of others. It is hard enough to live our own lives, as such everyone is better served if we concentrate on our own individuation, rather than being stuck in the agenda of others.

If the meaning of life is directly related to the scope of consciousness and personal development, then the invasions of the shadow at halfway are necessary and potential healing. The more I know about myself, the more of my potential I can incarnate, the more variegated the tones and hues of my personality will be, so too will be the experiences of my life.

It takes enormous courage to say that what is wrong in the world is wrong in us, what is wrong in my marriage is wrong in us and so on. But in such humbling moments we begin to improve the world we inhabit, and bring about the conditions for healing of both one's relationship, work and oneself.

TO RECLAIM WHAT WAS LOST

The appointment with oneself also means going back and picking up what was left behind, the untapped talent, the hopes of the child. If one could see one's own soul as a mosaic, one would not be able to count, let alone live, all the pieces, but each one affirmed heals and rewards the wounded soul. So the man who wanted to learn to play the piano or the woman who wanted to go to college or drift some summer afternoon in a row boat on the lake, can each do what was dreamt of and for whatever reason, left undone. We do not choose our psychic collection, but we choose to love or neglect its contents.

Yet many of us do not feel free to acknowledge our own reality. We lacked sufficient affirmation from the parent, or the example of a parents embrace for life. We internalised the neglect and the implied interdiction against living our potential. Seizing permission to live one's reality is essential after the fairy tales have come to an end. The fact that one is mortal, that time is limited and that no one will deliver us from the burden of responsibility for our lives, serves as a powerful incentive to be more fully oneself. As Seneca the roman stoic philosopher said, "You are scared of dying and tell me, is the kind of life you lead really any different than being dead?"

During halfway of our lives, the insurgence of the shadow is part of a corrective effort made by the self to bring our true selves back into balance. The key integration of the shadow and the unlived life, is to understand that its demands emanate from the authentic self, our true nature, which wishes neither further repression nor unlicensed acting out. The integration of the shadow requires that we live responsibly in society but also more honestly with ourselves. We learn through the deflation of the persona world that we've lived provisionally. The integration of inner truths, joyful or unpleasant, is necessary to bring new life and restoration of purpose, but more importantly ultimate meaning. When one has the courage to turn within, one has the opportunity to open up the neglected parts of one's personality creating an opportunity to the activation of one's own potential.

PARENTAL INFLUENCES

During halfway, it's time to become a child again, face the fear that power masks, and ask the old questions anew. They are simple questions, "What do I want to do?" "What do I feel?" "What must I do to feel right with myself?" These are the questions which must be asked and now is the time to keep the appointment with ourselves. We all must answer the questions as we're obliged to do. "Who are we?" "And what do I want to do with my life?" We can't resolve any such matters until we become conscious of the inner forces which block us, from the complexes acquired from our parents and from the storytellers. Any negative energy within us erodes our will, confidence and self-belief, but there's a much positive stronger force that represents empowerment, the capacity to engage in and fight for what one wants and the assertion of the life force. This positive energy is seldom given, it's achieved. Finding the courage to risk a new definition of ourselves is the task for all of us at halfway.

Perhaps no task is more important at the halfway point than the separation from parental complexes, for the simple reason that those powerful influences supported the false self and the fairy tales that held it all together. Until we can recognise the reactive rather than generative character of the first half of our lives, we're literally not ourselves.

There are a few parental complexes one must work through at halfway to rediscover oneself. At the most instinctual level, the experience of the parent was a primal message about life itself, how supportive or hurtful it was, and how warm or cold our welcome. How well or poorly did a parental figure mediate the child's natural anxiety? There lies the formation of the core angst which underlies all our attitudes and behaviour.

Secondly, the parent child experience constituted the primary encounter with power and authority. The imperative to find one's own authority at halfway is essential, otherwise the second half remains dominated by the vagaries of childhood. By what authority, that is, normative set of values, do we live? Who says so? Most adults spend half their time checking in. Thus, one must try to catch, render conscious all the conversations which go within. How many times does one consult or ask permission from the invisible presences in the head? The inner dialogue is more ingrained, more insidious than one might ever imagine. Who is the "me," who is actually "checking in," who are "they" Chances are those inner authorities are your parents or any form of substitute that represents a storyteller to you.

The reflexive character of this "checking in" is astonishing. It can only be combatted by noting when one feels distressed by a decision or conflict. When one is able to stop and ask, simply, "Who am I at this moment?" What do I feel? What do I want? Then one is not in the reflexive pattern but in the present. The insidious nature of "checking in" is that one is living in the past.

RELIGION

Religion dictates such a role for many people and they are infantilised by the lack of freedom to express their feelings without guilt. I've seen more damage than good done to people by authoritarian and unconscious clergy. Guilt and the threat of exclusion from the community serve as powerful deterrents to the development of the individual. It was no accident that the ancients considered exile the worst punishment which could be visited upon a person. Exile from the group is the great threat of authority.

No child can withstand exclusion from parental approval and protection, and so it learns reflexively to curb natural impulses. The name for that defence against that angst of exclusion is guilt. Without the ability to live in the present, to live as a self-defining adult, one remains a prisoner of the past, estranged from one's own nature and adulthood. To awaken to that inauthenticity is at first demoralising but ultimately liberating. How humbling it is to recognise the inner dependency on the outer authority projected onto partner, boss, family, friends, church or state. How frightening it is even in this day and age, to choose one's own path. The great tragedian Euripides once said, "The wisest men follow their own direction."

As a client just recently said, "I was told to consider myself was to be selfish. Even today I feel guilty when I refer to myself or use the word I." Many parents project their unlived lives onto their child. Classic examples would be the Stage-Door Mother or Golf Coach Father. A child often receives mixed messages from such a parent. "Be successful and you'll make me happy, but don't be so successful that you leave me behind."

It can seem a very fine line between lovingly protecting and nurturing a child, or living through the child inappropriately. When the parent has been blocked by anxiety for example, the child will find it hard to overcome barriers and may get stuck in an unconscious loyalty to the Parents level of development. But a parent who is living his or her life is not unconsciously jealous, not projecting expectations and limitations onto the child. The more the individuated the parent, the freer the child.

So the same freedom to become ourselves, we wished our parents to bestow upon us, we must grant to our own children. We have had to be ourselves and we often wish our parents had recognised that we were meant for different paths from the outset.

INNER VOICE

We all must seek to promote the inner dialogue, trusting that the voice of the self, will manifest and we can hear and trust our inner truth. This inner voice and to hear its mysterious call, is the beginning and the unfolding of which is the purpose of our lives. Just as we should treat our children, worthy of being different, having no obligation to us whatsoever. They are not here to take care of us, we are here to take care of us. As George Carlin said, "Parents are burning these kids out on structure. I think every day all children should have three hours of daydreaming. Just day dreaming. You could use a little of it yourself by the way. Just sit at the window, stare at the clouds. It's good for ya. If you want to know how you can help your children: leave them the fuck alone!"

So what is it that your called to do? By halfway no one needs to be made aware of economic reality. By the time we've all hit midlife one has surely learned the truth of the cliché that money will not buy happiness even as the majority will worry about impoverished retirement. According to a recent American newspaper to meet the realities of life, most of us will work jobs they hate to do. It's actually eighty-seven percent of people that dislike their work and only forty per cent that will change their careers. There's only a small percentage in the work force that find their work emotionally sustaining, while for the majority the dream of retirement beckons like an oasis in the desert.

OUR CALLING

There's a huge difference between a job and a vocation. A job is what we hold to earn money to meet economic demands. A vocation (from Latin vocatus, calling) is what we are called to do with our life's energy. It's a requisite part of our individuation to feel that we are productive, and not responding to one's calling can damage the soul.

We do not choose a vocation, rather it chooses us, and our only choice is how we respond. One's vocation may have nothing to do with earning money. One may be called to nurture others, or be an artist in a time which does not reward art, but we are sustained by saying yes despite neglect, even rejection. I myself personally love to write, which gives me an opportunity to channel my creativity while enabling others to be themselves. It's never about the money but loving what you do, it's not rocket science. As Aldous Huxley said, "I want to know what passion is. I want to feel something strongly."

The voice within, calls us to a different place. This calling cannot be denied, or renounced and if you don't it's a failing to abide by the contract in which you have been summoned here. Our vocation is seldom a straight path, but a series of unfoldings, twists and turns. If you betray yourself, you've also betrayed individuation. But for vocation one does not ask, one is asked, and a considerable part of the meaning of one's life comes from saying yes when asked. The ego doesn't run life, it knows very little. It is the mystery of the self that awesomely asks us to become whole, and how we decide to spend our energy plays a significant role in our journey.

When we recognise and withdraw the projections that money and power represent, then we are obliged to ask in radical form. "What am I called to do?" This question must be asked periodically and we must listen humbly to the answer. We may, in our individuation process be called to incarnate many kinds of energy. Just when we have achieved a measure of stability, we may be undermined from below and called to a new direction. Whatever our social burden, whatever our social constraint, we must keep asking anew, "What am I called to do?" Then with planning, the paying of dues and sufficient courage, we must find a way to do it. The sacrifice of the ego, with its need for creature comforts and security, is painful, but not half so much as looking back on our lives and regretting that we failed to answer the call.

The calling is to become ourselves as fully as we are able, the task is to find how. We are judged not only by the goodness of our heart, but also by the fullness of our courage. Relinquishing security we have struggled to obtain maybe frightening, but not as much as denying that larger person we are called to be. The soul has its needs, which are not served well by pay checks and perks.

Nothing will be achieved at the halfway of our lives, if we cannot discern the origin of those primary messages derived from our parents, and the storytellers. At midlife we feel a lot of distress, some from the outer, more so from the inner. Most of the inner distress originates from the fact that we and our society have colluded in neglecting the whole person. We have coasted on what was easy for us, we were rewarded for productivity, playing the game, yet not wholeness.

Our task is to live more fully, we can't grow up until we see our parents as other adults, special to our biography certainly wounded perhaps, but most of all simply other people who did not take on the largeness of their own journey. The storytellers fairy tales were put before us at the first leg of our journey, at halfway we've realised that being driven by wealth and status is to be caught in the web of the ego. To play the game of life by the rules of the storytellers which is an illusion. The ego won't fulfil you but it will edge out your true nature. To be free from the constricting need for social acceptance and to be oneself without the obsession of social comparison, is the beginning of going back to your originality. As Rollo May the American existential psychologist and author once said, "Every human being must have a point at which he stands against the culture, where he says, this is me and the damned world can go to hell." I totally and wholeheartedly agree.

DEATH AND REBIRTH

The privilege of a lifetime is to become who you truly are.

Carl Jung

"Midway in life's journey, I found myself in a dark wood, having lost the way." So begins Dante's spiritual pilgrimage, the alteration of his life's meaning, and so it is with you. The only requisite to entry into finding meaning in our lives is to have discovered that one does not know who one is, that there are no rescuers, no mummy or daddy, or knights in shining armour and that one's fellow travellers will do well to survive themselves. When one acknowledges one's arrival at this pivotal juncture, one may then be able to work through the warp and weft of one's life to find which threads lead from then to now.

T.S Eliot observed that our only superiority to the past is that we can contain it and be enlarged by it. The first half of our lives are full of expectations and we all arrive at midlife to find confusion, frustration and the exhaustion of the strategies that got us that far. Self-hate, anxiety, guilt and shame torture us which is the price we pay for internally not being courageous enough to question, query, challenge and follow our own inner compass.

To become aware of the signs that we're not ill or need to be medicated, but a cry from the growth forces from within. The neurosis we all suffer are our potentials yearning to be discovered which will create our meaning. These neurotic signals compel us to come to terms with what's going on inside of us and give us a better knowledge of our limits and potentials. Keeping our appointment with true selves involves both the suffering and the never ending search for meaning, it's only then that our growth is possible.

Through the first half of our adult lives we've reacted, namely to life's wounds. We've built a set of wound-based behaviours and lived out our handicapped vision with rationalisations, assumptions and expectations from the storytellers. Out of such wounds we create the assemblage of behaviours and coping mechanisms which serve to protect the fragile scared child within us. This assemblage, reinforced through the years, becomes the acquired personality, and our false self.

In the morning of our lives we lose our true identities to fit in with others, and in doing so play certain roles to keep up with the storytellers expectations and demands. We constantly try and justify ourselves, to those around us that to be the best, we have to do as we've been told and comply. Eventually we begin to realise that our nett value doesn't equal our self-value and the ego only limits and hinders our ability to see the truth within and what's important.

Alas we begin to learn we're just a small reflection of who we truly are. We toxify ourselves through self-medication and distraction and what we know about ourselves we do not love, we're repulsed, for what we see in the reflection in the mirror staring back at us is a stranger, a player, a manufactured product of the storytellers fairy tales. Without painful efforts towards consciousness, one stays wound identified. When we remain wound identified, one hates the reflection staring back and those that are responsible for the wounding are those we've listened to since childhood and adolescence.

The naivety we feel for not knowing better creates self-hate for one's frustration to break free from the programming and the status quo. These are the dark forces within us that have stopped us from being what we must become. This refusal to face up to our fears and remain passive has inhibited our capacity to live out our lives fully. As painful as the encounter with our shadow has been, it reconnects us with our humanity and our authentic nature. It contains the raw energy of life which, if handled consciously, can lead to change and renewal. As Sigmund Freud said, "One day, in retrospect the years of struggle will strike you as the most beautiful."

So out of our self-punishment comes our neurosis and ill health, but also the renewed vigour to be courageous and have an increased self-respect to do the right thing, to balance what has laid dormant within us. Growing and improving through our pain. As Kafka once wrote, "We all need a great work as it would be the axe to break the frozen sea within us."

If you're an artist you make music, you must paint, and poets must write. You must be true to your own nature as this is your contract with a higher power and you must hold your own promise to yourself. Your destiny represents your potential, inherent possibilities, which may or may not come to fruition. Destiny invites choice. As Abraham Maslow stated, "What human beings can be they must be." But for all of us to flourish as souls and to understand what optimises our consciousness, we must get rid of this nagging feeling that we're wasting our lives. And never go against our talents for example, if you're a painter and you're an accountant. The man who sees the truth but keeps his mouth shut. If you live like this you'll perceive yourself in the wrong way and have done wrong to your very being and despise yourself for it. From now on you must feel the thing you ought to be, beating beneath the thing that you are.

There's always an invitation for greater consciousness and an enlarged capacity for a more rewarding, enriching, meaningful life. With this comes a greater opportunity for forgiveness of others and of ourselves and a release from the past, so a rebirth may emerge.

One of the best things we can do after a rebirth is to let go of what no longer fits or is only adequate to the life stage you're in. You need to figure out for yourself what exactly is no longer appropriate as there's no list in the back of the book. But there is a hint that it can save you from considerable pain and remorse. Whatever it is, it's internal, it might be true that you emerge from death and rebirth with the clear sense that it is time for you to end a relationship or leave a job, but it simply represents the change that you're prepared to make. The transformation between death and rebirth begins with letting go of something that you have believed or assumed, in some way seen in yourself, an outlook on the world or an attitude toward others.

It is the internal things that really hold us to the past, and people who try to deal only with externals are people who walk out of relationships, leave jobs, move across the country. But who don't end up significantly different from what and who they were before. They are likely to be people who have not learned to change and avoid transformation. They storm out of a job ("rotten, no-good boss!") rather than let go of behaviours, attitudes, assumptions and images of self or others that keep making relationships turn out this way and their lives, tedious and robotic.

In making this important point, I don't want to leave the impression that psychological deaths never involve an external change, my point is simply that the inner ending is what initiates the transformation. You see change can lead to transformation, but transformation can also lead to renewal. We all have to experience an ending, you just can't keep fighting your experience. I can only conclude that you have to let go of something in the process. You may well need help, perhaps professional help, but you don't need me to tell you to stop crying over spilt milk and put on a happy face.

Let us just remember endings, are experiences of dying. They are ordeals and sometimes they challenge our sense of who we are and we believe they will be the end of us. Endings are the conclusions that terminates and it is too bad that we don't have better ways of reminding ourselves of this, the initiation of a process. We have it backwards. Endings are the first, not the last, act of the play.

But this is the moment of decision in our lives. Do we find courage in our lives to live a much more interesting and meaningful life facing our fears, or do we cower in the face of them. But the most flourishing among us are motivated to self-actualisation by the fulfilment of a mission of our own intrinsic nature. As Ernest Becker said in the book, The Denial of Death, "The safe road is the road of death, and if you do this you're as good as dead." Maybe it's time we become aware of our own death and the brevity of our lives and all of a sudden we won't waste it on the trivial or shallow and choose to move forward than remain trapped in a life that is toxic for our well-being.

Confronting your own mortality helps you get rid of the false, fragile and superficial values in life. As Mark Twain said, "A man who lives fully is prepared to die at any time." You can use death as the push you need to not pretend to be something you're not, just to fit in and conform to cultural expectations. As Virgil the Roman poet said, "Death twitches in my ear, "Live," he says, "I am coming."

I now want to share a folktale, "The Appointment in Samarra," that acts as a reminder that no one can escape death.

THE APPOINTMENT IN SAMARRA

The Speaker is Death

There was a merchant in Baghdad who sent his servant to market to buy provisions and in a little while he came back, white and trembling, and said, "Master, just now when I was in the marketplace I was jostled by a woman in the crowd and when I turned I saw it was Death that jostled me. She looked at me and made a threatening gesture, now, lend me your horse, and I'll ride away from the city and avoid my fate. I will go to Samarra and there Death will not find me." The merchant lent him his horse, and the servant mounted it. And he dug his spurs in his flanks and as fast as the horse could gallop he went. Then the merchant went down to the marketplace and he saw me standing in the crowd and he came to me and said, "Why did you make a threatening gesture to my servant when you saw him this morning?" That was not a threatening gesture, I said, "It was only a start of a surprise. I was astonished to see him in Baghdad, for I had an appointment with him tonight in Samarra."

The truth is death is coming right now. We don't have as much control over our lives as we've been conditioned to believe. Just because you're young, healthy and full of life doesn't mean you're protected from death. When you understand time is not on your side, you'll change the way you live from day to day because life won't change for you. As life exists with or without you.

Every now and again it's a good idea to take hold of your life and get a clearer perspective on how you live it and if you're using your time appropriately. I like to ask this question with my clients to help them to take a better look at their own lives.

Think of what would be unlived in your life if it ended today. Suppose you had a bad car accident right now or that you suffered heart failure, it's all over and your life is finished. Whatever you've done will be what goes down in the record books, and everything you might have done vanishes with the mind that considered it. Imagine that you are a family friend who has taken on the task of writing the obituary for the local paper or school magazine. Not your life story, but the things you did and didn't do with the years at your disposal. (Writing your obituary, is quite a revealing exercise) What would you write about yourself? Not your life story, but the things you did and didn't do, jot down some notes on a scrap piece of paper. You know, date of birth, parents, siblings, education, positions, honours, hobbies and then some last sentence, "At the death he (she) was…" (Was what? Was groping towards a new beginning, was stuck, was miles from home with darkness falling, was running scared, was done with trying to meet the expectations of others at last…was what?)

Endings are a death in one sense, the obituary is an appropriate statement about your past. As you think about that exercise, what do you think and feel about your past? What was unlived? What dreams, what convictions, what talents, what ideas and what qualities in you went unrealised? Are you are at a turning point now as the next phase of your life is taking shape? This is an opportunity to do something different with your life, something that expresses who you truly are in some significant way, it is a chance to begin a new chapter.

The experience of a death and rebirth is not unlike awakening to find that one is alone on a pitching ship, with no port in sight. One can only go back to sleep, jump ship or grab the wheel and sail on. This is no simple, "trip," but rather the journey of personal transformation that becomes possible after you have done the worlds business for long enough.

At the moment of decision, the high adventure of the soul is now more obvious. In grabbing the wheel we take responsibility for the journey, however frightening it might be, however lonely or unfair it may seem. But if we don't take responsibility and become accountable we'll still be enslaved by the storytellers fairy tales and live a false extrinsic existence which has never been our own. One of the most difficult tasks, is that of unlearning much of what we brought with us to life's middle years. And just what to expect before the transition of a death and rebirth. In my last book, "Learning to Unlearn," I wrote about this in some detail.

> *Your mind can fly to great heights but your parrot nature keeps pecking on the ground collecting knowledge that burdens the soul. Unlearn everything and embrace madness! Give your profit to the poor, forsake security, live dangerously, insult those who praise you, drink poison, and spill the water of life. Forget reputation, become a disgrace. I was prudent all my life from now on, I embrace madness.*
>
> **Rumi**

Just as were about to reclaim the inner kingdom of selfhood, home at last from the long journey, we discover not only that there is no welcoming committee on the dock to meet us but we must fight our way into our rightful place. So in the end, the homeward journey of life's second half demands three things. Firstly, that we unlearn the style of mastering the world that we used to take us through the first half of life, secondly that we resist our own longings to abandon the developmental journey and refuse the invitations to stay forever at some attractive stopping place and thirdly, that we recognise that it will take real effort to regain the inner "home." At no point do we live more honestly, or with more integrity, than when surrounded by others, yet knowing oneself to be alone, the journey of the soul beckons and we say "yes" to it all.

To live a more abundant life we are obliged to understand the limits within which we were raised. The implicit premise of our culture, that through materialism, narcissism or hedonism we would be happy, is clearly bankrupt. Those who have embraced such values are not happy or complete, yet still blinded by the fairy tales of the storytellers.

What we need is not unexamined "truth," but by going by our own heartfelt experiences, it is our own personal structure of intrinsic values and principles which will guides us in a way that is consistent with our true nature. While it is often useful to pick through the rubble of the past for images which speak to us as individuals, rarely is it possible to wholly embrace the mythologies and ideologies of another time and place. We are obliged to find our own.

The necessity of finding our path is obvious, but major obstacles stand in the way. Let us review for a moment the symptoms characteristics of a death and rebirth transition. They are boredom, repeated job or partner shifts, substance abuse, self-destructive thoughts or acts, infidelity, depression, anxiety and growing compulsivity. Behind these symptoms there are two fundamental truths. The first is that there is an enormous force pressing from below. Its urgency is felt as disruptive, causing anxiety when acknowledged, and depression when suppressed.

The second is that the old patterns which kept such urgency at bay, are repeated with growing anxiety but decreasing efficacy. Changing one's job or relationship does not change one's sense of oneself over the long run. When increasing pressure from within becomes less and less containable by the old strategies, a crisis of selfhood erupts. We do not know who we are really, apart from social roles, psychic reflexes, and we do not know what to do to lessen the pressure.

Such symptoms announce the need for substantive change in a person's life. Suffering quickens consciousness, and from new consciousness a new life may follow. The task is daunting, for one must first acknowledge that there is no rescue, no parent to make everything better and no way to go back to an earlier time. Our true nature has sought growth by exhausting the tired strategies of the ego. The ego structure, the conditioned self which one has worked so hard to create is now revealed to be petty, frightened and out of answers. During a transition the self, manoeuvres the ego assemblage into crisis in order to bring about a correction of course.

Underlying the symptoms that typify a death and rebirth is the assumption that we shall be saved by finding and connecting with someone or something in the outer world. Alas for all of those that experience a death and rebirth there are no such life preservers. We are in the sea-surge of the soul, along with many others to be sure, but needing to swim under our own power. The truth is simply that we must be courageous and that comes from within. If we can align our lives with that truth, no matter how difficult the abrasions of the world, we will feel healing, hope and new life. The experience of early childhood, and later of our culture, alienated us from ourselves. We can only get back on course by reconnecting with our inner truths and become reacquainted with what was lost from childhood.

> *"If you bring forth what is within you, what you bring forth will save you. "If you do not bring forth what is within you, what you do not bring forth will destroy you."*

THE GOSPEL OF THOMAS

What is within has been suppressed, we are ill and self-alienated. What is within has been so little affirmed, we have great difficulty in knowing that what we have sought all along, the path which is right for us, has been there. While it is frightening to contemplate the largeness of the task, it is also liberating in an ultimate sense to know that one has the necessary resources within and is not dependent on another to live one's life fully.

It is then a matter of living without those fairy tales once believed. For we are always guided by images, consciously, or unconsciously. Consciously we may subscribe to a set of beliefs and practices which accord with collective values, like the pursuit of wealth or acceding to group norms, but the price of such accommodation is neurosis. Or we may be living out a false fairy tale such as, "I must forever be the good child, eschewing anger and serving others." Neither out of conformity nor inner compliance supports wholeness. Indeed one is repeatedly enjoined to serve the outer, and when the collision occurs, to continue service to the programmed expectations. Again the stability of the society is served, but at the cost of the individual. In our lives we either choose fairy tales or the divine contract we all have been summonsed.

To be free from the constricting need for social acceptance and to be oneself without the obsession of social comparison, is the beginning of going back to our originality. Individuals don't look for the approval of social acceptance and determine standards of authority or how one should act, conduct oneself or live. To be free you must ask questions to your own conscious of what you need, and be willing to accept the truth and act on your truth. Hence we are all called to individuate which is the imperative of each of us to become ourselves as fully as we are able, within the limits of our own fate. Again, unless we are tied to it. We must separate who we are from what we've acquired, our false sense of self. "I am not what happened to me; I am what I choose to become." This sentence must be conscious to us each day if we are to become more than prisoners of our fate. As Montaigne said, "I have my own laws and my own court to judge me and I refer to these rather than elsewhere."

We will never know for certain how free or determined we really are, but we are obliged, as the existentialists reminded us, to act as if we were free. Such action restores dignity and purpose to the person who otherwise would continue to suffer only as a victim.

The ending of childhood is one part of the shift from life's morning (or dependence) to life's noon (or independence). A second part of that shift involves establishing a separate identity, distinct from that of being so-and-so's child. In traditional societies, the new identity was partly prescribed by your status and the clan that you are in. Partly discovered during the rite of passage, when some guardian spirit, ancestor or guru gave you a new name and a new sense of identity. With us, the old prescriptions have largely broken down, and we have fallen back on the idea that an identity is assembled during youth.

The psychologist Erik Erickson has explained how the process of identity formation works during youth, when a person tries on a series of roles and experiments with different kinds of relationships. Daughter, good athlete, average student, girlfriend, actress, sister, babysitter, shy person, closet moralist, dreamer, inventor, out of this potpourri of identities some coherent sense of self must be formed.

Each member of a tribal group moves straight from childhood into adulthood, but most modern people do not. Instead, in slowly changing forms, our dependency continues for some years. We eat the food our parents buy, we live in their house, and turn to them for help when we face some difficulty. But slowly all this changes, and then one day we finally are on our own. That is the next important transition point for most people, the time when we leave home and set up shop for ourselves.

We believe we are one's identification initially with the reality of our parents, and later with the authority of the parental complex and the fairy tales of the storytellers. As long as we remain primarily identified with the outer objective world, we will be estranged from our subjective reality. Of course we are always social beings, but we are also spiritual beings with a mysterious end of our own. While maintaining fidelity to outer relationships, we must become more fully the person we were meant to be. Indeed the more differentiated we become as individuals, the more enriched will be our relationships.

The paradox of individuation is that we best serve intimate relationships by becoming sufficiently developed in ourselves and that we do not need to feed off others. Similarly, we best serve our society by being individuals, by contributing to the dialectic necessary for the health of any group. Each chip in the social mosaic contributes best by the richness of its own unique coloration. We remain most socially useful when we have something unique, our fullest possible selves to offer.

Thus a concern for individuation is not narcissistic, it's a better way to serve society and support the individuation of others. The world is not set out by those who are alienated from themselves and others, nor by those who in their pain bring pain to others. It's about the person being the best they can be and offer who in turn contributes to the society in which they live, leaving it richer than it was before. The essential narrative is the opus which leads us to the Holy Grail, which is the goal of a lifetime.

When we grasp the wheel on the captains deck, scared not knowing our direction, knowing only that the thing must be done, then we live the high adventure of the soul. In the long run, it is the only journey worth taking. The task of the first half of our lives is to attain sufficient ego strength to leave parents and enter the world. This strength becomes available halfway for the larger journey of the soul. So a shift changes from the world outside to our world inside. From the ego to our true nature and the mystery of life unfolds in ever renewing ways. This is not a denial of our social reality, but a restoration of the essential unique character of who we are and what's more important to our story.

> *Is he related to something infinite or not? That is the telling question of his life. If we understand and feel that here in this life we already have a link with the infinite, desires and attitudes change. In the final analysis, we count for something only because of the essential we embody and if we do not embody that, life is wasted.*
>
> **Carl Jung**

The capacity to stand in relationship to that which is larger than our ego is to be informed and transformed by it. Over the entrance to the Temple of Apollo at Delphi, the priests inscribed the admonition, "Know Thyself" and according to an ancient text the entrance to the inner chamber had the collateral inscription, "Thou Art." These instructions capture the individuation dialect well. We are to know ourselves more fully and to know ourselves in the context of the larger mystery.

Each of us is called to individuate, though not all will hear or heed. If we do not tend to our own process, our own journey, we risk denying the life forces which led to our incarnation and losing our sense of meaning. As long as we are on the high seas of the soul anyway, why not be as conscious and as courageous as possible?

FROM LONELINESS TO SOLITUDE

"The best cure for loneliness is solitude," said the American poet Marianne Moore. What does she mean? What is the difference between loneliness and solitude?

Loneliness is not a contemporary discovery, nor is the flight from it. The jester was invented to divert the king from his loneliness, regardless of his position, if he thought of himself he would grow vexed and anxious. So it is today in our times with all the storytellers rhetoric and of modern culture distraction to keep us from loneliness and from thinking of what's important to us.

Similarly Friedrich Nietzsche wrote a hundred years ago, "When we are alone and quiet we are afraid that something will be whispered in our ear, and so we hate the silence and drug ourselves with a social life." Nothing has changed as this still rings true today.

The COVID-19 pandemic is in full force around the world and people for the first time in their lives are in total lockdown. Without their distractions that keep them company many are left alone for the very first time which is very scary and alienating for the majority of people. A lot of people don't want to be in a room by themselves as they are scared of what and who they'll find.

Sure, the introverts like myself welcome it, as I go and visit a little quaint, rustic cabin on top of a mountain for a week at a time to get away from a neurotic society. The culture, with all of its distractions and nonsense gives me the space I need to restore, heal, and return balance back to my true self. To help me gain perspective of my life and place with in it. I use this valuable time to acquaint myself with my imagination whilst being surrounded by the largest natural health tonic there is, nature.

But the majority of the population are extroverts and need constant human contact and distraction, through their five senses to keep their minds occupied and away from their inner truths. If distraction and resistance can't be found and delivered, depression and anxiety increase. The use of mental health services, have all skyrocketed since the COVID-19 pandemic which is a prime example of our dependencies on outer distractions and how we've become so addicted to what's outside of ourselves to ease and escape the pain with in. The storytellers have made it so convenient for everyone to fall into the trap of losing themselves into the world of technology and instant gratification. Which all have been designed to keep us away from our inner journeys and our true selves.

One cannot begin to heal or engage one's own soulfulness without a keen appreciation of the relationship to the self. To achieve this requires solitude, that psychic state wherein one is wholly present to oneself. We all must confront certain issues if one is to move from a state of loneliness to solitude.

ABSORBING THE TRAUMA OF SEPARATION

It is difficult to fully appreciate either the trauma of birth, which is a primal separation, or the full effects of the parent-child relationship. The more beneficial that relationship, the more one will be self-sufficient and comfortable with solitude. Paradoxically, the more troubled the relationship to the parent, the more dependent the person will be in their current relationships. The more volatile the parental environment, the more one learns self-definition only in terms of the other. It's amazing how much we have been defined by our parents and the parent substitutes such as social institutions, culture and digital media.

To move to the necessary solitude in which individuation can proceed, one must consciously ask each day, "In what way am I so afraid that I am avoiding myself, my own journey?" The co-dependent adult has learned to avoid his or her own being. The cliché, "To get in touch with one's feelings" really asks us to define ourselves from an inner reality rather than an outer context. Then we may operate out of personal integrity. The more traumatic the childhood, the more infantile our senses of reality. Risking loneliness to achieve that sense of oneness with oneself we call solitude is essential if one is to survive life and live it meaningfully.

LOSS AND THE WITHDRAWAL OF PROJECTIONS

Great losses occur along our paths, children move away, a friend dies, divorce shatters. The loss of that necessary other can be existentially terrifying as is the loss of the parent would be to the child. The adult feels not only angst but a loss of identity. What this tells us is how much of our lives have been caught up in the projections of meaning and identity onto the other, be it spouse, child or persona. Yes, some people feel liberated by a divorce or the departure of a child, but many do not. What is essential is to honour the relationship by feeling its loss, yet to recognise that one has had all along, a commitment larger than ones' self.

A person who has suffered loss and the withdrawal of projections will have struggled with the dependencies which haunt us all, but who will ask the next question, "How much of the unknown in me was tied up in that person or that role?" When we acknowledge loss and recoup the energy that was once invested outside ourselves, it becomes available for the next stage of life.

RITUALISING FEAR

People so fear loneliness that they will cling to terrible relationships and constricting professions rather than risk the consequences of letting go of the other. In the end there is no substitute for the courage necessary to confront loneliness. The "something" Nietzsche suggested we feared hearing may be useful and liberating. But we will never hear that inner voice unless we risk solitude. For some, it helps to devise a daily ritual of private meaning which obliges one to sit quietly, with no phone, no children, just nothing and listen to the silence. Such a ritual may at first seem strange and artificial, but sticking to it will allow the silence to speak. When we are not lonely in being alone, then we have achieved solitude. Fear keeps us from the essential meeting with ourselves.

The purpose of a ritual is to link a person to the larger rhythms of life. As they passed from generation to generation, rituals become routine and lose their original power. All the more reason then for the individual to generate a ritual of personal significance, investing in it with the same energy previously given to dependencies. The goal is to still the traffic to the mind, the neurotic clutter which floods and distracts. If we are afraid of being alone, afraid of silence, then we can never really be present to ourselves. Self-alienation is very much the condition of the modern world and it can only be changed by individual action.

So some part of everyday, it is good to risk radical presence to oneself, to follow a quiet ritual of disengagement from the traffic out there and traffic in here. When the silence speaks, one has gained companionship with oneself, moved from loneliness to solitude, a necessary prerequisite to individuation.

CONNECTING WITH THE LOST CHILD

It is not that we have a single child within, perhaps hurt, frightened, co-dependent or withdrawn in compensation. But a whole host of children, a veritable kindergarten, including the class clown, the artist, the rebel, the spontaneous child at one with the world. Virtually all have been neglected or suppressed. Surely this is one way to take Jesus's observation that to enter the kingdom of Heaven one must be a child again.

Certainly, we also have to deal with our narcissistic child, our jealous child, our enraged child, whose eruptions are often embarrassing and destructive. But we have more likely forgotten the freedom, the wonderful naiveté, the joy even, of life lived freshly. One of the most corrosive experiences of life is the sense of futility and joylessness that comes with routine, and frankly, the free child we all carry is seldom welcome at the office, perhaps not even in marriage.

So most of all, if we are to heal ourselves, we have to ask what our spontaneous, healthy child wants. For some the encounter with the free child will be easy, for others the work will be difficult, so deeply buried is this denied essence. But when we are stuck we are saved by what is within. If this free child is not approached consciously, he or she will break through unconsciously and often disruptively. It is the difference between becoming childlike, and in touch with one's inner child and being childish.

During a death and rebirth, one must finally ask that inner child what it needs, what it wants. Left behind by the manipulating and domestication of the storytellers fairy tales and fantasies is a natural orientation of the world and the many talents, interests and enthusiasms that go with it. We are rewarded for specialisation, not only at work but in intimate relationships. The talent left behind heals when brought to the surface and utilised. Given the colourful character of self, only a few facets will ever be lived. This incompleteness is part of the existential tragedy, but the more that can be lived, the richer one's life will be.

I've already noted that before a psychological death the flow of feeling is often blocked by boredom or fear. This is really saying that our own nature is too narrowly channelled and has become damned up. Where there is play there is life force. We all must emerge and act like children again, this is a need and hope to reconnect with what was lost at childhood.

To be reborn is an opportunity to ask, "What would my inner child enjoy?" Go back and take music lessons, take that art class, talent be damned, rediscover play. As a friend of mine who interviewed a number of retirees once said, "He never once heard the wish that one had spent more time in the office." We can still attend to outer obligations, work and relationships, but we must take time for the lost child.

THE PASSIONATE LIFE

Joseph Campbell the American professor of literature, would commonly say when asked how one should live, "Follow your bliss." He understood how most of the time we live according to the dictates of the storytellers, losing the best part of ourselves along the way. A lot of people have trouble with the word "bliss" as they equate it with narcissism or being to airy fairy. But I understand him to be referring to the inner journey, including all the suffering and sacrifice this involves. For me I believe to live with passion and to be able to create a life that pulls at the very depths of my inner core. Passion is what fuels our drive to live in the moment, and as the Greek novelist Kazantzakis said, "Leave nothing for death to take, nothing but a few bones."

Whilst experiencing a rebirth, we are invited to find our passion. It is an imperative to find that which draws us too deeply into life and our own nature that it hurts, for that experience transforms us. If we are here to be fully ourselves, then surely now is the time. There are commitments to honour, people whose lives are affected by our decisions and something to say for staying a course to which we have moral responsibility. Yet we are still obliged to live our passion lest our lives remain trivial and provisional, as if some day all would become clear and choices easy. Life is rarely clear or easy, yet choice is what defines and validates a life.

Fear of our own depths is the enemy as we do not feel we have permission. Authority is to be seized not requested as fear, not others, is the enemy. But if we are afraid of our own depth, or passionate capacities, we should be more afraid of the unlived life.

Here are some established truths:

1. Life without passion is life without depth.
2. Passion, while dangerous to order, predictability and sometimes sanity, is the expression of the life force.
3. One cannot draw near the Gods, the archetypal depths, without risking the largeness of life which they demand and passion provides.
4. Finding and following one's passion serves one's individuation.

When we become conscious of the largeness of our lives and reach beyond the confines of childhood and fairy tales, we then must say yes to our journey and risk all. Living passionately renews oneself when the old life has grown stale. Living passionately with love and understanding is the only way to love life.

THE SICKNESS OF THE SOUL

The whole psychological goal of death and rebirth is that of individuation and not the triumph of the ego. One of the grandest fairy tales of them all is happiness. A real state which one can discover and in which one can live permanently. Sadly, our life is more to wallow in the swamplands of the soul, victimised by sundry dismal inhabitants.

The natives in the swamp are loneliness, loss, grief, doubt, frustration, shame, despair, anxiety, guilt and betrayal for starters. But fortunately the ego is not the powerful commander it presumes to be as the soul has a purposiveness which lies beyond the powers of conscious control and our task is to live through these states and find their meaning. Grief for example is the occasion for acknowledging the value of that which has been experienced. Because it has experienced, it cannot wholly be lost. It is retained in the bones and in the memory, to serve and guide the life to come.

Rather than run from the swampland, we are invited to wade in and see what developing life awaits. Each of these swampland regions represents a current of the soul whose meaning can be found if we are courageous enough to ride it. When the ship at halfway is heaving in the swamp we must ask, "What does this mean to me? What is my soul telling me? What am I going to do about it?"

It takes courage to face one's emotional states directly and to dialogue with them. But therein lies the key to personal integrity. In the sickness of the soul there is meaning and a call to enlarge consciousness. To take this on is the greatest responsibility in life. We alone can grasp the ships wheel. And when we do, the terror is compensated by meaning, dignity and purpose. As Chuck Palahniuk said, "Only after disaster can we be resurrected. It's only after you've lost everything that you're free to do anything. Nothing is static, everything is evolving, everything is falling apart."

There is a phrase that I repeat often, "Memento Mori" meaning "remember that you must die". The phrase has its origins in ancient Rome, where it is believed that slaves accompanying generals on victory parades whispered the words as a reminder of their commander's mortality, to prevent them from being consumed by hubris. Yet today the storytellers have placed an emphasis with the transference of self-worth on the acquisition on to material acquisition and social status, modern culture has rendered death the enemy. Our western culture has a problem with the central fact of life, that we are all dying.

This obvious fact is fraught with implications. During halfway both the magical thinking of childhood, and the heroic thinking of our first adulthood before hitting half way, are replaced by the grim awareness of time and finitude. We are confronted with the fact that we're all getting older, life and what we wished for and wanted to live within the fairy tale becomes a stunned sense of our mortality. It's no wonder then, the older men who run off with "sweet young things" the women who have collagen treatments, the nip and tucks to hide the advance of time, the sweating and grunting at the gym. Fear of ageing and death animates these behaviours.

Why do we wish to remain young? It might be nice to trade in some body parts for more flexible ones, but why would one wish to step back into a sophomoric past? The answer is immediately clear, that one does not wish to take on life as a development, rather than a fixation that one is really not up to the fullness of the journey and would prefer to tarry awhile in the known and comfortable. So plastic surgery erases the epaulets of life's campaigns and adolescence rules the culture.

I've had the privilege to attend some who were dying more consciously than most, and as we get older a lot of our loved ones around us become ill and we have time to reflect on their lives. One of them was John who had been a client of mine. "I never thought this was going to happen to me, but it's the best thing that's ever happened to me, believe it or not." His ill health had summoned him to life. He had followed the rules by the storytellers and had led a responsible, good life but he had played the game he was told to, not the way he wanted to, and never knew himself until his illness. During his terminal illness he got in touch with those parts of himself that he had put on the back burner to follow the fantasies and wishes of the storytellers. John wrote a book, learned to draw, got in touch with his sensitive, intuitive self and counselled many who came to his bedside. I'll never forget John in his last 6 months as he had so much courage, strength and deep insight into his life. By the time he left this mortal coil, he was much larger than he was before his terminal illness as he had followed his journey with humility and an acceptance of himself. John had found the true meaning of life, which is to be true to who you are.

We become separated from our old identity and our old situation or some important aspect of it. So we float freely in limbo in between two worlds. But there is still the reality in our heads, a picture of the "way things are," which ties us to the old world with subtle strands of assumption and expectation. The sun will rise tomorrow, my mother loves me, the tribe will endure and the Gods are just: These things are so, and if they are not, then my world is indeed no longer real, we are disenchanted.

This may remind you of the disenchantments of your childhood: that there is no Santa Claus, that parents sometimes lie, are afraid and make stupid mistakes, and that best friends let you down. But our disenchantments did not end with childhood, nor are they over yet. Our lives contain a long chain of disenchantments, many small but a few large, lovers who prove unfaithful, leaders who are corrupt, influencers and celebrities who turn out to be petty and dull, organisations that violate your trust. Worst of all, there are the times when you turned out to be what you said (and even believed) that you were not. Disenchantments, you can quickly discover, is a recurrent experience throughout the lifetime of anyone who has the courage and trust to believe in the first place.

The suffering of disenchantments during a death and rebirth can be transformed. Ironically what is gained in a perspective on loss, for relinquishing old ego certainties, opens one up to a much larger reality. If we were immortal, nothing would really matter, nothing would really count. But we are not immortal, so each choice matters. It is through making choices that we become human and find our own personal space of meaning.

Many significant transitions during a death and rebirth not only involve disenchantment, they begin with it. But like the other aspects of the transformation process, it may be that the person can only slowly begin to see the disenchantment experience as meaningful. When you discover the fatal love letter or get the news that you've been fired, it's pointless to talk about realities. But later, it is important to reflect on these things, for with realities as with identities and connections, the old must be cleared away before the new can grow. The mind is a vessel that must be emptied if new wine is to be poured in.

The lesson of disenchantment begins with the discovery that if you want change, real change and not just to switch positions you must realise that the most significant part of your old reality was in your head. The flawless parent, the noble leader, the perfect wife and the utterly trust worthy friend, are an inner cast of characters looking for actors to play the parts. One person is on the lookout for someone older and wiser and another is seeking an admiring follower, and when they find each other they fit like the interlocking pieces of a puzzle or almost. Actually, the misfit is greater than either person knows, or even wants to know. The thing that keeps this misinterpretation in place is an "enchantment," a spell cast by the storytellers by the past onto the present. Most of the time these enchantments work fairly well, but at life's turning points they all breakdown. Almost inevitably we feel cheated at such times, as though someone were trying to trick us. But usually the earlier enchanted view was as "real" as we could manage at the time. It corresponds to a self-image, a situation that it could not change without affecting ourselves and others.

The point is that disenchantment, whether it is a minor disappointment or a major shock, is the signal that things are moving into transition. At such times, we need to consider whether the old view or belief may not have been an enchantment cast on us in the past to keep us from seeing deeper into ourselves and others than we were ready to. For the whole idea of disenchantment is that reality has many layers, none "wrong" but each appropriate to a particular phase of intellectual and spiritual development. The disenchantment experience is the signal that the time has come to look below the surface of what has been thought to be so. It is the sign that you are ready to see and understand more now. To see life as it is.

We know we have survived upheaval and disruptions to our lives when we no longer cling to who we are, no longer seek fame and fortune or the appearance of youth. The sense of life as a slow taking away and the inexorable experience of irreplaceable loss, is transformed by relinquishing the old ego attachments and affirming one's deepening descent into the mystery. As Jesus said thousands of years ago, "That to win life we must learn to lose it."

The paradox of our lives is that only through relinquishing all that we have sought, and adhered too by the storytellers do we transcend the delusory guarantee of security and identity. Then most strangely, surplus of existence floods our heart. Then we move from the knowledge of the head, important as it sometimes is, to the wisdom of the heart.

For those who worry about the impact of their journey on others, we need to remember that our best way of helping them is by living our own life so clearly that they are free to live theirs. No one can say where the journey will take us. We only know that we must accept responsibility for ourselves, that the path taken by others is not necessarily for us and what we are ultimately seeking lies within, not out there. As the grail legend suggested centuries ago, "It is a shameful thing to take the path others have trod." It is only from within that we perceive the promptings of the soul and it is this emphasis on inner rather than outer truth that distinguishes the second part of our lives from the first.

The act of reaching a higher state of consciousness and potential, is central to living a life of meaning and purpose. The conscious experience of being human and going through the psychological death to a rebirth is about separating who we are from the sum of our experiences we have internalised. Our thinking then moves from magical to heroic to being human. Our relations with others becomes less dependent, asking less of them and more of ourselves.

If our courage holds, the next part of our story brings us back to life after we have been cut off from it. Strangely for all the anxiety, there is an awesome sense of freedom as well. We may even realise that it doesn't matter what happens outside as long as we have that vital connection with ourselves. The new found relationship with the inner life more than balances losses in the outer. The richness of our inner journey proves to be a voyage worth taking.

Creating identities made us identifiable to others, but we no longer need any validation from out there, as we now know it's what's inside our hearts that count. As Soren Kierkegaard said, "The biggest danger is that of losing oneself." But now you've chosen to become identifiable to yourself and have given yourself the authority to embrace your own true nature. To create a life all of your own and to write your own script.

The storytellers all want us to have identities as it means fame, and fortune, it means power, prestige, wealth and status, all the trappings of the ego. It's the illusion that you're above everybody else, making you feel that you have a sense of entitlement. But it's when you oppose these forces and no longer play along with what's expected, you've reached a high level of freedom. Great heroes sometimes won combats simply by scaring off their opponents. I am Hercules, I am Achilles. To say, "I am a nobody" and to find in that a new non-identity, a source of power, that is something significant and it marks a stage of development going beyond the reliance on roles. As you no longer need to try or uphold cultural expectations or the collective story. The greatest moment in your life is when you become comfortable in your own skin, without any labels. To be yourself, is to be a nobody which is a lot less tiring and a much more rewarding experience.

BE A NOBODY

The game is not about becoming somebody, it's about becoming nobody.

Ram Dass

The first question were likely to encounter in a new meeting with somebody is, "What do you do for a living?" According to how you answer this question, you'll either become the centre of attention or you'll be left alone by the appetizers. How insane and stupid does this sound, but how often than not does this occur at a social gathering. It's ironic as I know successful people from society's standards who are extremely wealthy but are so dull and serious that being around them is as painful as having your teeth pulled out. It has been said at times, "Have you seen who God gives his money too?" Regardless of what you have an abundance of materialistically, it won't make up for ones' character, passion for life, wisdom, or depth and substance. A pretender is really anyone who takes a small part of you and uses that to come to a universal and rigid sense of who you are. The kind of pretentiousness that is dominant in the world today, is not around bloodlines, lineage or how high you are on the upper echelons of society. But what job you have and in particular how impressive your powers of financial accumulation. According to that criteria people will judge you immediately, so it's often said, "That we live in a materialistic world." We simply live in a world where material accumulation has become the gateway to the respect and love that we all crave. Just another fairy tale woven by the storytellers.

None of those who have been raised to a lofty height by riches and honours is really great. Why then does he seem great? Because you are measuring the pedestal along with the man. A dwarf is not tall, though he stands in a mountain; a colossus will maintain its size even when standing in a well. This is the terror under which we labour and how we are deceived; we value no man by which he is, but add the trappings in which he is adorned.

Seneca

It's not really the riches and the fast cars, large houses or the overseas vacations taken every year. But it's the honour and love if you like, which are a conduit to perhaps the only channel to a different way of looking at so called greed. The next time you drive and those times you walk down the road and you see somebody driving a Ferrari don't think this is somebody who's greedy, who's materialistic. Think first and foremost this is somebody with an incredible intense need for love. Who has not been able to find the honour and respect they need in normal ways and therefore they're needing so much more stuff in order to feel they have the right to exist.

If you can deal with just riding a bike through your neighbourhood and that's okay something's gone right in your past. If you're a parent and your child has no ambition to become famous you're doing something right. As that means, this person is able to deal with being themselves without too much other stuff. One of the most beautiful but also dangerous ideas in western culture is the notion that anyone can achieve anything. So we hear these messages from everywhere that is the spirit of what we've been brought up with by the storytellers. It may seem like a beautiful message but it's a dangerous message, because if you really believe in a world where you can do anything and you've only done a bit your only something. Heaven forbid how crushed will you feel. The possibilities for humiliation are so much greater now and have become so detrimental to our psychological well-being.

If you go into a bookstore and you look at the self-help section there are basically two kinds of books on that shelf. The first is a book that tells you how to make a million dollars in an afternoon and the other book is telling you how to cope with low self-esteem, and the two books are totally related. If you live in a culture telling you how to make a million dollars in an afternoon, but you won't be able to your going to have massive self-esteem problems. So how can you achieve esteem of yourself when you're going to be part of the ninety-nine percent, and not the one percent who actually become extremely affluent.

Most of us are going to have an ordinary life. So what have we done believing in a world in which an ordinary life is not good enough. This is crazy, this is a form of self-torture. We've now created a life where an ordinary life is materially more comfortable than it's ever been. In an ordinary life you're going to get a good car, you're going to be able to have a shower every night, you're going to have a roof over your head, and more importantly you're going to have pretty nourishing food. So materially an ordinary life is terrific. But then we've put a snake in the grass, we've ruined paradise that we've built and our ancestors have built for us. By telling ourselves that actually contrary to everything we hoped for, an ordinary life is psychologically not good enough.

It's not good enough just to drive an ordinary car, have an ordinary house and have an ordinary shower once a day and have an ordinary meal. No that's not good enough you need to be extraordinary. Become Elon Musk become somebody else right, this is a kind of torture that we've imposed on ourselves which is totally insane. How have we made a life where the statistical odds of you leading that life, which is a ninety-nine percent surety that you will lead that life has come to seem like a humiliation and the wrong sort of life. This is setting yourself up for a surety of mental instability.

> *Culture is a perversion. It fetishes objects, creates consumer mania, it preaches endless forms of false understanding in the form of squirrelly religions and silly cults. It invites people to diminish themselves and dehumanize themselves by behaving like machines.*
>
> **Terrence Mckenna**

If we could raise our state of awareness enough and be clever about it, we could build a society for ourselves, a society for nobodies. Interpreting our lives in a way, unlike most of our western counterparts that most of us are going to be normal. So we can make schools for nobodies that are going to be fantastic and trains for nobodies that are going to be beautiful and amazing kindergartens for nobodies. I'm using the word nobodies to define actually most of us, the ninety-nine percent who are going to be, well just normally average. We are all of us almost fated and in every area of life, that we will encounter failure. We're fated to be ordinary, nobodies. An ordinary life is a good life and let's not torture ourselves, and believe that the only way to be good enough is to be somebody, rather than an ordinary nobody.

> *I'm sick of not of having the courage to be an absolute nobody.*
>
> **Jerome Salinger**

This is poison and look don't get me wrong, a bit of ambition is fantastic, a bit of get up and go is great we're not in any danger of being unambitious. The danger now is suicide. I'm putting it at its deepest and darkest. The danger is that we will feel so inadequate in relation to the expectations and standards of the storytellers fairy tales, that we may choose to end our own lives. This is happening in huge numbers, as we as a society are suffering from an epidemic of mental fragility, or as I put it earlier as a sickness of the soul. Largely bred by our assumptions that our lives will be stellar. When in fact they are more likely only to be ordinary and we'll only ever be nobodies and not somebodies.

Too much expectance of ourselves has made us sick. Meritocracy as I mentioned earlier is based on the idea that people will get what they deserve. If you really believe in a world in which those that get to the top deserve to get to the top. You're going to be believing in a world in which those who are at the bottom deserve to be there. So being poor and so called unsuccessful moves from being a problem to being a condemnation, of your society on you. You know you move from being an adventurous unfortunate to being a loser. It's incredible punitive so no wonder people take that very badly and they do. So we don't need any more reminders from any influencers on instagram or anyone else to get up and go and be a winner. We've heard that message and it's making us sick. We know it's so well, we know it to well, and we need to hear another message.

That message is you're okay just as you are, it's okay to fail, it is okay to be ordinary, a nobody. It's okay not to know what's going on. It's okay to be lost in a universe most of whose recesses will be always darkness to us. Joy is not going to be making five million dollars. Joy is going to have a drink with a friend, sharing a heartfelt moment with someone special, joy is going to have a meal that turns out okay. Happiness is going to be a day at the end of which, no one has died and there's been no crisis it's been more or less alright. Love is not going to be perfection, love is going to be occasionally a hand held by somebody who understands bits of you, never the whole of you but has charity towards your darkest moments. This is the life the majority of us will lead, and from this moment on let being nobody be your power to enjoy an ordinary amazing life. Let's all be nobodies and revel that it's okay to accept ourselves as we are.

MEANING

There is no greater agony than bearing an untold story inside you.

Maya Angelou

Throughout our stories we've learnt that life's not easy and obviously not a fairy tale. For all of us to free ourselves from the illusionary chains which have bound our feet since childhood from a mould of living which has suffocated our authenticity. We've all had to emerge from the darkness and break free from the collective structures which have kept us from being true to ourselves. Unless we all can emerge from the darkness, with new purpose and a better understanding of our lives and what's happened to us, no change will take place. We have learnt that those things that hurt, instruct and to transcend our disorientation into meaning we must firstly have an awareness and skill to confess our grief and frustration so healing can transpire and we can become whole once more.

For us to lead better lives we have to achieve a better understanding into what governs us to further the dialogue consciously and subconsciously. We must learn a new skill of identifying what will make us more harmonious with our inner core and how we can reconnect with what has been lost. Meaning is only found from insight, and only through our own self-discovery can our deep wounds be healed, so new growth can transform from the very fractures that gave us pain in the first place.

The narratives of our lives and what it means to be happy and successful have created such heavy burdens. Perfectionism, unreasonable standards, competition, animosity, shaming and devaluing of our better qualities. These capacities have come at a hefty cost to those we love and to ourselves. This burden has always been there, but as we get more insight into our lives we become more courageous and begin to question the necessity of living under the myths of a fairy tale. So we can begin a new and create a chapter of our own. As Henry David Thoreau said in Walden, "In short I am convinced, both by faith and experience, that to maintain one's self on this earth is not a hardship but a pastime, if we will live simply and wisely."

> *We are all born free, bearing the term of wholeness and health, and then life happens. Since children are dependent upon their parents and their culture for the fulfilment of basic needs, they are quickly estranged from that natural being. We are all socialised to serve and maintain the collective, family structures, social structures and social institutions that have a life of their own but require the repeated sacrifice of the individual to sustain them.*
>
> **Jacques Rousseau**

Within our bones and the fabric of our nerves and the corridors of memory, we carry this child still within us. But what happens to that child, afraid to be itself? Still living in the moments of spontaneity, in an impulse of joy and delight. The dreams of yesteryear slip from awareness as we head off to work. The child lives deep down within, suppressed and weary, heavily laden with myths that don't match our reality.

Wanting to come out and explore the child desperately hopes for information, for modelling, for leadership, for instruction, for help in coping with what eventually confronts us all and perhaps overwhelms us. When we undertake such trials, we hope that they will take us aside and teach us what we need to know. But to our surprise they never take us aside and tell us what it means to be yourself. To enjoy your individuality and true nature or how to conduct yourself in a way that best serves your own unique character and well-being.

Now I realise of course that the storytellers of my time, my parents and those that I've listened too, respected and admired, did not know what it meant to be a fully functioning individual and adult. They similarly were uninitiated and could hardly pass on the mysteries and liberating knowledge they themselves lacked. They only knew from their level of consciousness and understanding.

So we stumble blindly through the necessity of rites of passage from childhood to adulthood. Not only are such rites about transition from the dependencies of infancy to the self-sufficiency of adulthood, but equally the transmission of such values as the quality of being a good citizen within the community and those attitudes and beliefs that connect us to our soul, to our society and meaning. Yet such rites passed away a long time ago.

A rite is a movement in and towards depth, which creates substance. Rites are not invented, they are found, discovered and experienced. A life without depth and substance is hollow, life is an experience and the purpose of a rite is to lead us into or back toward that experience of depth. Without meaningful rites we sustain the most grievous of wounds to our true nature, and a life without substance. The idea of a passage is similarly essential, for all passages imply something ending, or a death of sorts and something beginning, or a birth of sorts. Only death is static, the principle of life is change, and we have many deaths and rebirths to transit if we are to lead meaningful lives. Initiation implies entry into something new, something mysterious.

The majority of us don't go through any initiation process as such, given the fact that rites of passage have largely disappeared from our culture. For what is not available through our culture we are now obliged to find for ourselves. It seems that our predecessors had intuited the importance of such separations and evolutions of personality as they collectively grasped that these processes were necessary. The duration, intensity and decisiveness of such rites were in direct proportion to the difficulty of truly leaving childhood and growing up. As few in our culture have managed, psychologically speaking, to separate, to grow up, it may profit us to reflect awhile on the stages of initiatory experience. Again what is not provided to us by our culture is left to us to do as individuals. We cannot avoid the task through ignorance, for otherwise the developmental process of becoming an adult remains undone.

James Hollis wrote a book called, "The Middle Passage." In it James describes this developmental process as follows. It's brief but it gives you a good understanding of the rites of passage we all need to be psychologically and spiritually prepared for being a balanced human being and to live a meaningful life.

1. **Separation.** To separate from the parents, this is a physical separation to prepare for a psychological separation. To stay in the comforts of the parents, with warmth, nourishment and protection to remain with the parents, whether literally or figuratively, is to remain a child and to give up one's potential as an adult.

2. **Passage of death.** This is a symbolic death of childhood dependency. We suffer the loss of home. It was the loss of innocence and the loss of childhood.

3. **Rebirth.** If there is death, then life must follow. This is the emergence of a new being.

4. **Teachings.** Imparting such knowledge as the youth would require in order to function as an adult. To be able to survive out in the world, the privileges and responsibilities of adulthood and citizenship were similarly transmitted. Also an introduction to the mysteries, so the young person would have some spiritual grounding and participation in the transcendent realm. "Who are our Gods?" "What sort of society, laws, ethics, spirit gifts, did they bestow?" Locating the person in a mythic context bestowed identity, gave a sense of the greater framework in which they participated, and deepened the soul of the youth.

5. **Ordeal.** The youth is required to suffer a separation from the comforts and protections of familiar surroundings. A journey to a sacred space away from the community or isolation away. The essential part of being an adult means not only that one

can no longer turn backward to the projection of other, but one must learn to draw upon inner resources. No one knows they have them until they are obliged to use them and our suffering quickens consciousness. Without some form of suffering, physical, emotional or spiritual, we are content to rest easy in the old comforts and the old dependencies. No matter how large or confronting our ordeals, we realise regardless of how large our tribe, we are on this journey alone and must learn to draw strength and solace within, or we will not achieve adulthood. We all must learn to depend on our wits, courage, strength or perish.

6. **Return.** The child is now an adult, and is prepared for living life, with what one has experienced through the rites of initiation.

The elaborateness of the traditional rites of passage is necessary then, to bridge the huge gulf between childhood and adulthood or between a child's instinctual life and dependency and the independent self-sufficiency of adulthood. If the rites worked, the person experienced an existential change, they died as one being and became another. But as we all know, such rites today are missing, such existential transformation has been driven underground. If you ask a person, "Do you know yourself?" Chances are they'll consider the question silly or threatening. They'll know their roles, but they won't be able to define what it means to be themselves. In short, the wise elders are gone, lost to death, depression, alcoholism or corporate boardrooms and golden parachutes. The bridge as it is from childhood to adulthood is washed out.

As people we have no meaningful rites of passage available to us, no wise elders to transmit what lies on the other side, we have necessarily had to take clues from societal role expectations and essentially hollow role models. All the while, pain and confusion to our true nature is repressed within and acted out violently, or distanced from our consciousness. The gap between wisdom and experience has been filled by outer images, images which seldom feed the soul. As Terrence Mckenna said, "The major adventure is to claim your authentic, true being, which is not given to you. The culture will not explain to you how to be a real human being. It will tell you how to be a banker, politician,

Indian chief, masseuse, actress, whatever, but it will not give you true being."

Doing what your true self wants rather than societal role expectations, and marketing, advertising, digital media, our parents, education, religion, ideologies and our culture, is risky business. As we get to this point in our life we see that stepping into a larger life is intimidating because it requires that we risk being who we are, that is, what wants to come to the world through us, rather than serving our ego comforts or whatever fairy tales, societal expectations or cultural infections which have plagued us. We cannot expect someone else to give us permission. Those ideologies, or the cultural complexes, are embedded in history, and never will stop saying what they always have said, as they possess a stunted imagination. So it's up to us at this later point, when we have served those voices for so long, to realise that our own souls have a unique point of view. That each of us is different, and are bound for different stories and at the end of our life, we'll have to answer as to what we did with our summons.

We must step into our largeness and acquire our own personal authority, rather than the authority of the storytellers, and live this life with risk and courage. A friend of mine used to run a church group and would often tell me she would hear the phrase, "And what is it we believe in this matter?" To me the saddest thing is most people don't question or have any of their own thoughts on issues that have an importance to them and need to ask frequently, "What is it I believe?" Do they ask advertisers, "What is it I should buy?" I believe they do.

Fear is the enemy, most of all fear of largeness. The largeness of our own true natures which is most intimidating and is why we defer so often to the instructions of the storytellers. Every Sunday morning I see people flocking into their local congregation of worship and being told what their values should be. In Australia tens of thousands flock to large auditoriums to listen to their coiffed gurus, what their values should be and how they are to live their lives. I don't see a summons to the large risk of the true self or an enlarging encounter with mystery. I do not see such banalities honouring the Gods and their terrible powers. I see it as an infantilising repetition of the obligation of childhood, to serve voices of outer authority, obeying and giving up one's own sovereignty. To reinforce the recrudescent message that one's wellbeing derives from obeying the powerful other. The "Other" that also lies within us, the voice of our true self seems then, so impossibly far away.

We've all learned and been raised to run from the idea that the Gods brought us here to carry out their will, whatever that maybe. Rather than serve the troubled timidity of our mutually neurotic culture. Yet, when we spin our journey from our deepest places, we find a continuity of intention, a steady feeling of support that allows us to cross over the abyss of existential angst. Then we discover that what we feared most was our own terrible, insistent freedom and to write a script of our own.

Choosing to risk one's own authority, to step into this fearful place, to realise through experience that one will be supported by something deep within each of us, is what brings us home to ourselves. After all the fear of largeness begins by fearing the resident largeness that is our own souls. If we can abide that fear of ourselves, we will not be afraid of others. So when you've faced your own demons, the demons of others will not frighten you. But I've seen time and time again how quickly one of the ways we defend ourselves, against the depth and complexity and yes the craziness of ourselves, is to split it off and deposit craziness onto somebody else. Facing our own abyss opens us to acceptance of the magnitude of the other as well, whether found in a relationship, nature, or in a mysterious movement of the Gods themselves.

Every day that we can call out those demons of fear and reductionism and step into the large journey intended by the true self, we actually serve the world better by bringing to it the unique gift that each of us represents. How could denying our gift to the world ever really serve it? Stepping into our largeness and creating meaning for ourselves is not narcissism, it ultimately proves our greatest contribution to others. All it requires is the resolve to stand humbly but responsibly before our own largeness and then step into it.

Just remember you are a loving human being and a great soul. Please sail your boat out into uncharted territory, towards new horizons as new meaning and experiences await you. The past is the past and the trail of your boat is behind you. Realise the wake of the boat doesn't steer your boat, you do and it isn't were your life is lived but only in the present moment. The future with new friends, relationships and challenges is rushing towards you, asking that you be ready for it. It will ask much of all of us as we are summoned to be willing participants in the making of this future.

The roles, ideals and unrealistic societal standards which have been enforced to us by the storytellers, rest heavily upon us all. If we continue to blame them, and those who spoke and created fairy tales, invented and institutionalised all of this, then nothing will change. We can no longer wait for something to change out there, we all must learn to change ourselves. All change starts within, but as people we often have trouble internalising our experience. So the task is difficult, but it is far preferable than living under the spell of a fairy tale.

We are not here to be comfortable, although that is the banal blandishments offered by the storytellers and the modern materialistic culture. With all its seductions of addiction and distraction as Chuck Palahniuk said, "The only way to find true happiness is to risk being completely cut open." In the end we must become more comfortable with our uncertainty, a mystery driven life, more than certainty ever would.

HOMECOMING

Going home means coming back to ourselves after so much estrangement.

Luke Sheedy

Those venerable sages knew that the story the ego was living, the fiction it embraced, was not the true story, hence the deep sorrow and nostalgia we all carry for a lost home. That lost home is ourselves, but how do we make it back there? Paradoxically, we can only make it back home to ourselves by going forward into the unknown and scary possibilities of a risky, more fully lived journey. Each of us is aware of the many places where our story beckons and we have known for some time, but we have mostly managed to avoid stepping into it.

How does one go home without going back to an earlier place, a place that cannot be recovered and whose delusory seductions lead to regression? In using the word nostalgia (which from the Greek word means "pain for home") one risks the sentimentality of returning to a safe familiar psychology and of a staying stuck in someone's else's story. Perhaps the most seductive of all going home fantasies, is to find the magical other through whom we feel nurtured, protected and kept from our journey. Whatever our story maybe and that is for us to discover, it will be suffering, risk, anxiety and often great loneliness. No wonder we prefer the simpler past.

For all of us to go back home to our true selves, we have to separate ourselves from other people's stories, especially those of the storytellers. It's time to depart and head towards the discovery of our own personal authority. Sure we can learn alternative stories, it can be useful from mentors, gurus and therapists which they can offer, but we cannot find our authority to live our journey and encounter the mystery of this journey through them. We have to discover for ourselves, some authentic narrative which has already been written deeply within ourselves. The keys to unlocking the doors to go within are aplenty, our bodies, our intuitions, our reflections, insights, dreams and visions.

We've always had the keys in our pockets metaphorically speaking, but we've learned to distrust them while adapting to and obeying the clamorous claims of the world. But seen or not seen, they are always there, announcing a summons to open our journeys to a larger world. When such keys are neglected, something in the soul dies, goes underground and grieves, or enters the outer world as a projection that tricks the eye, diverts us into empty amusements or distractions, or sends us chasing spiritual will-o-the-wisps.

Going home means paying attention to and respecting the witness of these clues. It asks that we risk taking them seriously and it means tracking the clues to see where they wish to take us, which will not necessarily be where we wish to go. Going home means coming back to ourselves after so much estrangement. So long have we been strangers in this world, and so long strangers to ourselves. How scary, how inviting, how necessary it is to come home at last.

Imagine what your story would look like if, rather than succumbing to the persistent voices of family or culture, we determined that our vocation was to be a better human. Many, if not most of us, will have run through our lives and never really been here. Never really experienced precious moments of mindfulness, asked why, or felt ourselves in the presence of mystery, whether found in the beloved, in nature, in contemplation, in the work of the hands, or in whatever venues mystery comes to find us. What matters is that we become who we really are.

> *Your problem is how you are going to spend this one and precious life you have been issued. Whether you're going to spend trying to look good and creating the illusion that you have power over circumstances or whether you are going to taste it, enjoy it and find out the truth about who you are.*
>
> **Anne Lamott**

When we are here to live an authentic life, we can spontaneously be generous to others, for we have much to give from our inner abundance, as we can draw and maintain boundaries. For we have learned the difference between their journeys and ours, so we can sort through different value clashes because we have found a personal authority that helps us discern what is authentic for us. In short, we have recovered a relationship to the soul from which we lost contact, but that nonetheless continues to hum beneath the surface of our lives and never, ever loses contact with us. We learn the truth of T.S. Eliot's lines that, "The end of all of our journeys is to arrive at the beginning and to know it for the first time."

I truly believe we all have appointments to keep, appointments with others to be sure, but most of us all, appointments with the meaning of our own journey. Why are we here, why are we sucking air, and are we adding to or subtracting from the world. Many people from which I have noticed, do not show up for their appointments. When they do not, whose life are they living? That of the storytellers! When did they get off the path meant for them by the Gods? Childhood!

We all get off the path for a while because we are tiny, dependent, ignorant and afraid. Thus after the fairy tales have all been dissolved usually around the second half of life, if we are granted one by fate. Is about getting back on the path, our path, whether approved by parents, the storytellers, endorsed by the consensus of our tribe, comforting or not. Only a person who has been on the road and has been themselves and experienced failure, know they're living their lives and not somebody else's.

By then, they've learned that the task is not to find the object, but to be true to oneself, to live the journey, with passion, risk, commitment and danger. It has nothing to do with the seductions of shiny objects, status, success, or arrival. For some of us, the risk of loving another in the face of our forbidding history provides our journey. For others risking a talent, an enthusiasm or an imaginative summons, is our journey. What gives us our journey also gives us our home, our richness and our meaning.

Personhood is not a gift, it's a continuing struggle, as the gift is attained later and only from living a mindful journey where, prompted by an inner summons, we write our story at last.

Life is too short for games unless it's a game of cards. Don't text back right away: if you like them, pretend you don't: and don't you say I love you first. Well screw all that. I will text you back in three seconds: I will tell you that I like you: and if I love you, I'll tell you every chance I get. Life is unpredictable, and I'd rather play every card as honestly as I can than have a deck full of regrets and what-ifs.

Courtney Peppernell

BIBLIOGRAPHY

Becker, Ernest. *The Denial of Death*. Simon and Schuster, 1997.

Bridges, William. *Transitions*. Da Capo Press, 2004.

DeBotton, Alain. *The School of Life*. Penguin Random House, 2019.

Hari, John. *Lost Connections*. Bloomsbury, 2018.

Hollis, James. *The Middle Passage*. Inner City Books, 1993.

Janikian, Michelle. *Your Psilocybin Mushroom Companion*. Ulysses, 2019.

Kierkegaard, Soren. *The Sickness Unto Death*. Penguin Books, 2008.

Maugham, Somerset. *The Appointment in Samarra*.

Ramey, Mark. *Studying Fight Club*. Auteur, 2012.

Sheedy, Luke. *Learning to Unlearn*. Inner Knowing, 2019.

Storr, Will. *Selfie*. Picador, 2017.

Watts, Alan. *Eastern Wisdom Modern Life*. New World Library, 2006.

www.ingramcontent.com/pod-product-compliance
Lightning Source LLC
Chambersburg PA
CBHW071917290426
44110CB00013B/1387